The Agnostic Faith Trilogy

A Loveforce Trilogy, Three Book Paperback

Finding God without Religion, The Best Spiritual Quotes,
Finding God in A Chaotic World
By The Prophet of Life
Book 1
Finding God without Religion. An Agnostic Path To God
You and Your Path to God, in Life and Beyond
Revelations of 2012 Book 2: You & Your Path To God: In Life and Beyond

- You & Your Path
- What Defines You
- Fulfilling Your Destiny
- Life Lessons
- Your Perception Determines Your Reality
- Spiritual DNA

- The Nature of Suffering and Sacrifice
- The True Meaning of Failure
- The Nature of Addiction
- Finding Your Gifts
- The Path To Heaven
- The Fine Art of Dying
- What Happens When You Die
- Psalms
  - Beyond your perception
  - To Be Loved
  - No Time To Cry
  - Born To Win
  - The Gift
  - Everybody Makes A Difference
  - When The Spirit Moves Me

Book 2
The Best Spiritual Quotes
by The Prophet of Life

Spiritual Categories:
Spirituality
Mercy
Life Lessons
Life
Knowledge
Inspirational
Humanity
Heaven & Hell
God
Faith
Fear
Death

Book 3

Revelations of 2012

Finding God in a Chaotic World

Chapters 1-11 & Psalms

Preface

Sample Excerpt: Introduction…My God

The Nature of The Lord

The Lord Is God of The Universe

The Lord Communicates with Everyone

The Lord Loves Everybody

Religion & Enlightenment

God is Portable

The End Is Not Near

The Paradigm Shift

In The Beginning

The Messenger

If You Want To Get Closer To God

Psalms

All Contents Copyright 1979, 1980, 1981, 1986, 1987, 1990, 1991, 1993, 1994, 1995, 1996, 1997, 2006, 2007, 2009, 2010, 2011, 2012, 2013, 2014, 2015, 2016, 2017, 2018, Loveforce International Publishing Company. All Rights Reserved.

Preface

We are proud to offer our readers this Agnostic Faith Trilogy in paperback form. This single volume combines three superb books by The Prophet of Life, one of the most powerful and profound voices of faith in the New Age. In Finding God without Religion he provides an agnostic path to God. In Finding God in A Chaotic World, he shows you how to find and recognize God, how God communicates with you and how to get closer to God. In The Best Spiritual Quotes he provides you with further food for thought and contemplation with spiritual quotes that will enlighten and help you on your journey. It is our hope that our readers will find enlightenment and joy within the pages of this volume. If you know any Spanish speaking readers who would be interested in the topics in this book, we also sell a Spanish language version of this paperback.

Sincerely,

Evan Loveforce
Coordinator,
Loveforce International Publishing Company

Finding God without Religion. An Agnostic Path To God

You and Your Path to God, in Life and Beyond
Revelations of 2012 Book 2: You & Your Path To God: In Life and Beyond

Preface

A spiritual person can find God just as easily as a religious person. An Agnostic can find God just as easily was a religious person. You don't have to be religious to find God because religion is not God, it is man's interpretation of God. In reality God communicates with everyone including you, it is just that many people either aren't aware of this or don't know "how" God communicates with them so they don't think it is God that is communicating.

Many people join a religion because they need the structure or because they want to be "saved". Many religions tell you they have an exclusive path to God. This is not true. Religions are often founded, based on the teachings of a particular prophet. God reveals information to humanity in increments over long periods of time that correspond with humanity's development. Humanity gets what it needs and we learn a little more each time.

There is nothing wrong with people joining a church or a religion but remember the church and the religion are not God. If you want to find God search within yourself. Look at your life and figure out when God has been communicating with you. Find out what God's messages were and you can trace the path of your successes and failures in life depending on whether or not you followed those messages.

---The Prophet of Life

1 You and Your Path

"We are all on separate journeys through our life experience. No matter what our faith or beliefs, we take this journey as individuals."

Welcome to your life. Your life is a journey. On your journey you will encounter joy, pain, good times and bad. Wonderful things will happen to you. Horrible things will happen to you. You will cherish the ones you come to love. You will lose the ones you love. You may even lose yourself for a time.

In the time that you are here, in the time that you are taking this journey, you will be faced with many choices. Some you will make wisely, others you will make foolishly. Still others will be made for you, by others, by happenstance and by unseen forces. This is all a normal part of your experience here. All who live must go through both positive and negative experiences. All people have control over some experiences. All people have no control over other experiences. You cannot always control what happens to you but you can control how you react to it, how it affects you and what you learn from it.

On your journey you will be presented with different paths that you can take. Each path will take you to a different destination. You will be given opportunities to change the path you are on. You will be given warnings. You can always make adjustments and change course. Where you end up will be determined by your ability to hear, heed and correctly react to the warnings you receive and the choices you make. What you take away from your journey will depend on your ability to learn from your mistakes and to grow into a spiritually balanced being.

2 What Defines You

"What society tells you defines you is not what defines you."

We must all work to earn our daily bread. The average person has an average job either manufacturing something, or servicing something or someone. The wealthiest people don't have to work, and some don't, but many do. They either have a corporation or a legacy they are responsible for maintaining. Those with a lot of money can choose how they spend their time and also sometimes choose the type of work they desire to do.

People who are homeless and living on the streets, they work too. They must do something to raise monies needed for their sustenance. They often beg. Begging is the hardest work of all because a beggar is totally dependent on the whims of others. Work is important but work is not who you are. It is just a means to an end. Some enjoy their work, others are consumed by it. Work however, does not define you.

We must all live somewhere. Many live where they can best afford to. Some live in upscale neighborhoods, in large houses. Others live in a cardboard shack. Everyone finds the best location they can to live and raise their children. Where you live does not define you.

We must all eat and drink. People eat and drink whatever is available to them according to their location and budget. People buy the best food they can with the money they have to spend. Some eat processed foods. Others have an all-natural diet. Things that are easily available in some parts of the world are not available in other parts. You must eat. What you eat can affect your health but what you eat does not define you.

We all learn. We learn at school, at home and on the streets of our neighborhoods. We learn from information we receive from a myriad of different sources. We learn from our life experiences. Some are university educated. Others learn only from experience. We all learn but what you learn and where you learn it doesn't define you.

These four things, your work, your residence, your food and your education are the building blocks of survival. What we eat, where we live, how we work and where and what we learn, are not the building blocks of life. The building blocks of life consist of what you believe and what you do.

What you believe defines you because people are ruled by their belief systems. What you believe can influence what you do. What you believe in and how you believe it defines you. The things you do and the spirit in which you do them define you. What you believe and the actions you take on those beliefs are what define you.

3 **Fulfilling Your Destiny**

"Every being has a destiny. Are you fulfilling yours?"

Every human is born with a destiny. At birth, God whispers the same phrase to every person "The world is a better place because you were born." The phrase is a prophecy. It is a prophecy that proclaims part of your destiny. It is a prophecy you are charged with fulfilling during your lifetime.

Part of your life mission is to find out how your life can fulfill this prophecy. There are many ways you can fulfill this prophecy. You can fulfill it through a lifetime of service to others. You can fulfill it discovering, creating or inventing something that benefits the world. You can fulfill it by saving the life of another living being.

You can fulfill this part of your destiny through service to others. Many professions, from doctors, to firefighters, to teachers to garbage workers can help fulfill God's prophecy. Most people can understand how doctors, firefighters and teachers are included on the list because doctors and firefighters are perceived as saving lives. Teachers are perceived as saving the future by educating children. Far fewer may understand how a garbage worker can be included on the list. Garbage workers help with diminishing the effects of disease. Many garbage workers become sick from diseases clinging to the refuse of people who are sick. In doing so, they contract an illness that many others might have contracted if the garbage was left out in the open in a public place.

You can fulfill this part of your destiny by discovering, inventing or creating something that benefits humanity. You can discover the cure for a disease. You can invent a machine that helps to clean up the environment. You can create a painting or a sculpture, a poem, rap, piece of music or song that uplifts people's spirits or gets them to think about the big questions of life. Any of these types of activities can make the world a better place, one soul at a time.

You can fulfill this part of your destiny by saving the life of another being. Saving the life of a person could enable that person to complete their fulfillment of this part of their destiny. Saving the life of another being, a plant or animal for instance, is performing an activity that creates a direct effect for the being you are saving and future generations of that living being's descendants.

Most people are not artists or writers. They cannot create an artistic or literary masterpiece. They are not doctors, or teachers. They live ordinary lives working mundane jobs for less money than they think they are worth. They can save a life, if not the life of a person, then the life of a plant or an animal. They can volunteer to help at a hospital or an orphanage. They can be help a stranger in need, they can join groups like Change Agents for Humanity to get ideas on what they can do.

The question is clear. Will the world be a better place because you were born? The answer may be unclear because in most cases, words alone will not satisfy it. Only your actions will create an answer to the question. What actions are you taking? How is the story of your life answering the question?

4 Life Lessons

"Life is a never ending series of lessons."

The Lord speaks volumes to each of us. Most of us never listen. There are many times in our lives that we are given opportunities to learn life lessons. Sometimes they are presented to us as things that are told to us, seen by us or that happen to us. We are meant to learn from them. Life lessons, however, go beyond our own experience. We must also learn from the experiences of others. We often see people, some that we know, others that we do not know, making mistakes. We are meant to learn from their mistakes as well.

Someone you know might say or do something that has dire consequences for them. Sometimes the event that befalls them is the crescendo of a series of bad decisions and stupid, impulsive acts. Other times, it is the result of one catastrophically bad decision or act. The child who touches the hot stove and burns their hand, the teenager who beats another and ends up in jail or the adult who drives drunk and runs over somebody all should learn a lesson themselves but so should those around them. In the grand scheme of things, sometimes people who suffer dire consequences are meant to serve as an example and / or a warning for others. Those who do not learn from others mistakes may be bound to repeat them. Those who learn from the mistakes of others may be saved from the consequences that befall others.

As each person is supposed to learn from their mistakes, so too are communities of people. Whether these communities are neighborhoods, cities or nations, they must learn from their mistakes and the mistakes of others. The mistakes of ourselves and others have been handed down for millennia in the form of oral and written histories. There is a direct correlation between mistakes made by communities (many of them now extinct) in the past and what communities in the present and future do. Knowing the history of your own people as well as that of other people can broaden your community's horizons and can provide more possibilities for solving problems. There are many peoples in this world but in reality there is but one race, the human race. Humans must learn from the mistakes of the human race and not be confined to studying the trials and tribulations of one segment of it.

So study. Study people and events in your daily life. Study events in the local, national and international news. Study the histories of various cultures. The lessons are there for you to learn from. The broader your education is, the more well-rounded your knowledge and experience is. The broader your education, the more enriched is the Soul you return to The Lord.

5 Your Perception Determines Your Reality

"Change your perception and you can change your reality."

Two different families lost their homes. They both downsized and moved into an apartment. Both families have a breadwinner. The perception of each of these two breadwinners had a profound effect on the outcomes of these two families.

The breadwinner of the first family blamed others for his situation. He grumbled and complained about his misfortune to anyone who would listen. In a short time, people who were his friends walked the other way when they saw him because they were tired of hearing his complaints. He became bitter and saw little hope for any improvement in the future. It scarred him deeply that he could not provide the little extras for his family that helped make life more bearable. He dragged himself to work every day, resentful that he had been repeatedly passed over for the promotion that would raise his fortunes up from the quagmire he was living in and might have prevented him from losing his home in the first place. His grumbling, resentful nature affected his performance at work. In a few months he was let go from his job. Soon after that, he was facing the very real prospect of becoming homeless. He saw no hope for any improvement in the future. He feared the thought of being homeless. He felt like a total failure. The day after the eviction notice came, he killed himself. His wife and two children were left having to face homelessness without him.

The breadwinner of the other family was initially devastated by the loss and his friends also know what has happened to him. He didn't dwell on it though and looked at the loss as an opportunity to learn from mistakes he made so he wouldn't make them again. He looked for something to be happy about every day. He often found at least one thing to be happy for each day which made him see the good things in his life. This made him grateful for the blessings he did have in his life. When he went to work, he was his usual positive cheerful self. Some of the people at his work knew what he had been through and his ability to stay positive in spite of his circumstances made them sympathize with him. When a chance for a promotion came up his boss realized that he had come through a difficult time and it hadn't affected his excellent performance. He was given the promotion. He was frugal with the extra money he made and saved a good amount of it so he could afford to put a good down payment on another house. Within a couple of years, he and his family bought another home.

    Why did one breadwinner find success and the other perish? Simply put, it was their perception. While one breadwinner blamed others for their misfortunes and saw things through a completely negative light, the other sought out the lesson in their misfortune. They learned from the lesson and followed through by following the knowledge gained from the experience with the appropriate actions.

    Life is a series of learning experiences. The Ups, the downs, the triumphs and tragedies are all meant to teach lessons through the experiences they yield along with the potential lessons that are available for those who are looking for them. How often have the mighty been brought down? Some are brought down for good, others are brought down only to arise again stronger than before.

How often have the greatest triumphs arisen from the ashes of the greatest tragedies? The greatest triumphs are those which are the hardest to conquer. Many times they demonstrate the real strength of the human spirit. They can also be the greatest teachers.

Since people live their lives as a member of the human community, you don't even have to go through the tragedies yourself. There are lots of opportunities to learn from the experiences of others whether you read about them, see them on T.V. or in a movie or witness an event yourself.

Even though the lessons are all around us, so many people don't realize that there is a lesson to be learned. This is because they are not looking for lessons outside of a formal classroom at an institution of learning. They don't realize that life is a classroom and everything that happens to you, everyone you know and everyone you see or hear about is a potential lesson.

So many people spend their lives chasing after dreams of fame or fortune. They invest their time and their money to hone a skill or talent that they believe will help them achieve their goal. Some of them even achieve their goal but unless they have learned the lessons their life experiences were meant to teach them, they don't achieve the happiness and fulfillment that comes with finding your true calling. They aren't able to hold onto the fame or the money because they have not developed the life skills necessary to weather life's storms.

The truly wealthy people in life are those who learn the lessons their life experiences are meant to teach them. Many of them are successful in whatever endeavors they undertake because they learn from their mistakes and grow beyond them. If they lose everything, they have the foundation to weather the storm and the faith to believe that success will come again. They also have the knowledge to put together a plan to arise from the ashes and the gratitude to be happy with whatever they have which helps sustain them through the sacrifice needed to put their plan into action.

6 Spiritual DNA

"Just as your body has a physical DNA, your Soul has a Spiritual DNA."

Besides their physical DNA, all living beings have a spiritual DNA. Spiritual DNA is what connects your soul from one incarnation to the next. Further, it connects all incarnations of the same soul to each other. Spiritual DNA can allow living beings to connect with good things and bad things from previous incarnations.

The good things from previous incarnations can include talents (like playing a musical instrument) or proclivities (like either knowing or learning a foreign language with uncharacteristic ease). Those who are creative may also "picked up" things from previous existences. Just as people have motor memory, they have spiritual memory. Some creative people may be calling up things recollected from past incarnations, either that they may have created themselves or experienced. There are a great many things created by civilizations past that are lost to us historically but not spiritually.

The bad things people can connect with can include phobias, traumas and negative déjà vu. Phobias can include things like fear of water (drowning) and heights (falling). Traumas can include unexplainably severe reactions to things like minor vehicle accidents, or extremely adverse reactions to medications or minor illnesses. Negative déjà vu can occur when one has uncharacteristic reservations about entering a place or interacting with a specific person or group of people.

Physical DNA allows traits from one family member to be passed on to another family member born later. Spiritual DNA works similarly but Spiritual DNA and physical DNA do not work together. A soul reincarnating sometimes reincarnates into the same family but doesn't always.

Characteristics from Spiritual DNA are much less pronounced and often much more difficult to bring out. In this way, a great baseball player, who dies shortly after the birth of his son may be able to pass on certain physical characteristics to that son but often cannot pass on the experiential facets contributing to his success because he didn't reincarnate as his son.

Not all souls have chosen to reincarnate, some have not chosen to have an incarnation at all. All souls have existed since the dawn of time but not all have incarnated since the dawn of time. What each soul has learned from each incarnation is extracted and enriches that which is God. That which is learned does not refer to talents or what is learned through reading and studying, it refers to what each soul has learned about life, humanity and the state of the various species encountered in its incarnation. There is, however, some spiritual residue which remains and that enriches each Soul's Spiritual DNA. It is that residual information which people can and many do, occasionally tap into.

Some beings, like Prophets for example, are linked across different Souls through Spiritual DNA. Such beings have an awareness of each other's incarnations and are among each other during their individual incarnations. They can call upon each other for strength and guidance during their individual incarnations. They influence and assist each other when they are not in an incarnation state.

Prophets differ from other beings in that the God Gene in their Spiritual DNA allows them direct access to direct communication from The Lord. This is to assist them in their mission. This is necessary because in the entire myriad of generations which have existed, so few Prophets are incarnated. The Lord communicates to humanity in increments over long periods of time. Prophets need the extra assistance in order to get the message out and sustain it over time. Prophets are not better than other people. They are merely different. While all living beings have a purpose and mission unique unto them, prophets have a mission to inform humanity. They have chosen to be incarnated solely for this purpose. They may have other things they do in their incarnations but informing humanity is their focus.

Just as Science began unraveling the mysteries of physical DNA centuries ago, science can now begin to unravel the mysteries of Spiritual DNA. Science doesn't study things until they are thought to exist. Until The Lord revealed the existence of Spiritual DNA (among other things) in this volume, it wasn't known to humanity. Now that it is known it can be delved into. It will begin with discussions as to whether or not Spiritual DNA exists. It will evolve into hypothesis and theories about it and then to designing experiments to prove or disprove its existence and eventually evolve into unraveling its mysteries until spiritual DNA is as well understood as physical DNA is today.

7 The Nature of Suffering and Sacrifice

"Suffering and sacrifice can teach lessons that can lead to enlightenment."

Suffering is a state of being which is accentuated by one's emotional state of being and / or ego. Life will present many opportunities for suffering but suffering is only as bad as you allow it to be. Suffering can be either minimized or intensified by how you react to it.

Suffering is a part of life. It is meant to build character. In these times, it often builds bitterness, resentment and hatred. Suffering can be your greatest teacher if you know how to learn from it. It is through suffering that you learn what you don't like and have an opportunity to make the changes that will eliminate the suffering. Listen to your suffering, analyze what is its cause and work on correcting the cause.

Suffering is also a state of mind. Pain can be very real but there are two types of pain, physical and mental/emotional. The mind and spirit can minimize and sometimes eliminate them both. The annals of history are filled with those who have gone into a trance state and been able to overcome physical pain. Mental and emotional pain can also be overcome. Life is filled with setbacks, disasters and accidents. Many have a certain proclivity towards wallowing in self-pity. This only lengthens the time and effect of the suffering. Focusing on potential solutions instead of focusing on crying about the problem can help minimize suffering.

In the grand scheme of things, suffering is meant to teach a lesson. Whether the lesson is meant for an individual, a group, a culture, a nation or a planet depends on the suffering. The nature of suffering is that it shall continue until the lesson is learned. Sometimes it takes a lot of repeating until the lesson is learned. Both good and bad people reap the benefits of the sunshine. Both good and bad people receive rain for their crops. Chaos and disaster befalls both the good and the bad. The difference in the aftermath of tragedy is the lesson learned or not learned. The nature of suffering is that it shall continue until the lesson is learned. This is true for an individual, a community, a nation or a planet.

Sacrifice is denying oneself something for the purpose of advancing forward towards a planned outcome or goal. This can work for an individual goal (like atonement or spiritual enlightenment), a familial goal (saving money for your child's college, stopping smoking so you can live long enough to see your child go to college) or a community goal (like cutting down on pollution through recycling).

Sacrifice is also meant to build character. It also teaches lessons. Beyond this, sacrifice helps achieve goals. It has an end product which is tangible. Going without something or with less of something one day, could mean that it will be available another day. This speaks directly towards conserving resources whether they are resources of the individual or of the planet.

While there is rarely a need for suffering (other than catharsis, building character or teaching a lesson), and suffering can be minimized by ones personal outlook, there is often a need for sacrifice. People who squander what they have over a short period of time or who act as gluttons, hoarding and pigging out on resources often end up resourceless or friendless or both. Life is a long haul. It takes sacrifice to make it to the finish line.

People who do not sacrifice often become selfish. Communities who do not sacrifice often find themselves out of resources. Societies who do not sacrifice, rarely achieve anything worth noting.

8   The True Meaning of Failure

"Success often arrives on the coattails of failure."

Have you ever failed at anything? Of course you have. If you are like most people, failure is a common occurrence. Not because everybody completely sucks but because failure is a part of the learning process. If you are like me, you probably fail at most new things you try. If you keep on trying however, you get better.

Do you know how to walk? Can you talk? These are things you learned as a baby. When you were a baby, you took your first few steps and fell and fell again but you kept on trying. You were likely curious about this new mode of transportation your mommy and daddy were using.

What would have happened if you gave up on walking? Can you imagine what your life would be like if you had to crawl everywhere? You didn't give up. You kept on trying and learning from your mistakes and making correction and now, you are walking like a champ!

There can be no success without failure. Success is often a matter of trial and error. What scientists call error, the rest of us call failure. Failure is an opportunity to learn. You learn what doesn't work. You can either believe that the whole thing doesn't work, you can't do it and likely never will and give up or you can try another way.

Failure can be the key that unlocks the door to success. Besides learning what doesn't work, failure can teach you what went wrong and why it went wrong. If you analyze a failure and trace all of the steps you took leading up to it, you can see just where you went wrong and once you knowing where you went wrong often leads to knowing how and why you went wrong. Knowing where, how and why you went wrong can give you information that allows you to make corrections, corrections that will lead to adjustments that in time will lead to success. The information yielded from failure can be the keys that unlock the door to success.

9 The Nature of Addiction

"Addictions may present themselves as your path but they are actually dangerous detours."

We spend a part of our lives leaning on crutches. Crutches are things that we lean on. They can manifest themselves as addictions. People can be addicted to substances like drugs or alcohol. They can be addicted to diversions like gambling, pornography, sex, sports or physical activities.

For some, addictions can be the focal point of their lives, the thing around which the majority of their existence is centered around. For others, it is merely part time diversion which they can hold at bay most of the time. Many addictions begin as part time diversions but build up momentum over time until they become all consuming.

Many people have addictive personalities. They become easily addicted to something. The addiction they choose can either cause partial or catastrophic damage depending on what the addiction is and how much they allow it to take control of their lives. People throughout history have controlled addictions through sublimation, switching a very bad addiction for one that is not as bad or to something positive.

Addictions can come from a need or longing that is unfulfilled. The need can be physical, mental or emotional. There are many circumstances that are beyond your control in your journey through life. Sometimes these situations can cause a need or longing to take control back. This need can start you on the path towards addiction. Not finding love can cause sexual obsession / stalking behavior. Boredom can cause thrill seeking which could manifest itself as gambling or drug use. Feeling powerless over your life and / or problems can cause drug and alcohol use in an effort to medicate your pain away.

People who are addicted get several warnings about the escalation of their addictions. These warnings can come from concerned friends and family or from circumstances that those addicted find themselves in as a result of their addiction. Those who are addicted to something must first realize that they are addicted and decide to make a change. What is often helpful for many addicted people is to work within a community of others who are similarly addicted, recognize it and have made a commitment to change, to end the addiction. In the time that this has been written these are known as 12 step programs.

10 Finding Your Gift(s)

"The gift is in your thinking, the power in the dreams you dare."

You have a purpose and a mission in life. On your path towards enlightenment you will need to find your gifts. Everyone has special gifts. Some can fix anything. Others can play a difficult concerto perfectly. Still others have an uncanny rapport with wild animals. Some gifts you acquire on the journey, others you are born with.

Do you know what your gifts are? Think of the things you do well or the things you somehow adapted to extremely easily. They could be as easy to identify as a special talent (like singing) or difficult because of their subtlety (like being able to communicate in a way that is understood by different kinds of people). You might try asking friends and relatives what they think are your strengths or what they admire about you.

Look back at your life and identify things you have been successful at. Try to link the strengths you and others have identified with examples of things you have accomplished as a result of using those strengths. The things you have accomplished don"t have to grand just identifiable. For example, someone with mechanical ability might have identified what was causing a minor problem with their dad"s car and fixed it, thereby saving their dad some money on a repair bill. This could illustrate how someone using an identified ability (mechanical) benefited their family (saving money on the cost of a repair).

Make a list. On one side of the paper write your identified strengths and on the other write successes or benefits obtained by using them. List some goals you have in life. Look at your strengths. Then, try and ascertain how you can use your gifts to assist you in achieving your goals. If you are ever wavering about which goal to try to accomplish, try looking at each goal in the context of how many of your strengths can be used to help you accomplish it. The goal that has the most of your strengths needed to accomplish it could be the one that will be the easiest for you to accomplish.

11 The Path to Heaven

"If you want to enter heaven, leave your ego at the gate."

The Lord loves religion. The Lord loves religious people. Deeply religious, pious people are not only people who stand up for their belief in The Lord they are also the pillars of any community they are a part of. People who are deeply religious have an advantage when it comes to getting into heaven. Their religion provides them with a way to enter heaven. They believe it and when they die, their spirit can use it. Their religious belief provides them with a path to Heaven.

For 99% of the human race, the path chosen by their religious belief is the path used. Each religion has its own path to heaven, governed by its own rules. Generally, your path to Heaven is governed by the rules that govern the path you choose while you are a guest here in this life and on this particular planet.

Despite what you may have read or heard elsewhere, there are many paths to Heaven. Others have claimed that their way is the only way to Heaven but this stems more from a desire to attract followers to their religion than from divine inspiration. Also remember, most Prophets who have come before me either didn't put their knowledge into written form themselves or most or some of their original writings have been lost to us. I am putting the things that I have been sent into written form but I know that in time, my original writings are likely to vanish or be adulterated by others after my time on this planet has expired.

The Lord is an equal opportunity lover. The Lord loves all souls despite the form of embodiment that they take in their life. Please remember that not all souls live in human form but they are still equal in the eyes of The Lord, even if humankind doesn't consider them equals.

Just as The Lord loves those who are religious, The Lord loves those who are not religious. There are a great many people who are affiliated with a religion and not practicing or are not affiliated with any religion at all. Do you honestly believe that a loving God could condemn them just because they never saw the light? If you truly believe that The Lord is the most benevolent being in the universe, how could you believe that everyone who was not religious was going to Hell? That every infant, child or person who died before they could get saved by a religion would all have to suffer the same fate despite the fact that they were either innocent or lived a righteous life? I wouldn't condemn them and I am not The Lord. Not condemning them would make me more benevolent than The Lord. The simple truth is, I cannot possibly be more benevolent than The Lord, and therefore, The Lord would not condemn them either.

Right about now, you may be thinking to yourself, "So where is the justice?" How can someone who has not been religious and pious all of their lives get into Heaven when they didn't put in the work that I did? The justice is in the essence of the soul and in the grand scheme of things.

All are judged by what they have been given from the start of their existence and what they have done with it. All souls come into this life imbued with certain talents and handicaps. They are born into certain environments. They are like raw materials in the beginning, and the sum total of their life at its end is the finished product.

All souls, in their purest form, journey from The Lord into this life. Souls in their purest form have, built into them a Spiritual Blueprint which knows the difference from right and wrong. This Spiritual Blueprint allows each soul the ability to have a conscience. This combined with the God Gene in their Spiritual DNA allows all souls to directly communicate with and receive direct communications from The Lord and have the conscience to prevent the living beings they are part of, from performing incorrect actions.

Incorrect actions are those which displease The Lord. Actions that do harm unto others in any way or form displease The Lord. This would also include standing by and allowing others to perform actions that harm others. The Lord loves harmony, tolerance and compassion. Those who are tolerant and compassionate tend to live in harmony with their neighbors. Harmony, tolerance and compassion must however, must be combined with courage, fairness and honesty. Those who are fair and honest and have the courage to stand up to others to insure that fairness and honesty prevail help insure that justice too can prevail. Someone who is tolerant and compassionate might tolerate a neighbor who beats his children for the sake of maintaining harmony with that neighbor. Someone who is tolerant, compassionate, honest, fair and courageous might have compassion for the beater but would also have compassion for the children and would have the courage to call in the authorities to make sure the beatings were stopped and the needs of both the beater and beaten addressed.

Souls in their purest form know right from wrong. They know what pleases The Lord. They are born into this life with talents and handicaps and into a particular environment. So, how do so many go wrong? The talents and handicaps combined with the environment and life experiences add a lot of extra baggage to the soul.

The complete soul of a living being has three parts which mirror an atom. There is a nucleus with two parts the Pure or Original Soul and the God Gene surrounded by a protective outer layer called the spirit. The Pure / Original Soul known as your Perfect Soul, is positively charged. The Spiritual DNA God Gene has no charge. The Spirit is negatively charged.

The purpose of the positively charged Perfect Soul is to record what talents and handicaps you have been given, informing your spirit what is right and what is wrong and determining what your spirit needs to do to return to The Lord's presence at the end of your life. The purpose of the non-charged God Gene / Spiritual DNA is to act as a conduit for direct communication with The Lord. The Purpose of your negatively charged, outer layer, spirit is to absorb the impacts that life experiences have upon you, thereby creating a unique individual personality but also protecting the Perfect Soul and God Gene from the impact of life experiences. Over time, your spirit can get clogged with all of the crap that your life experience has taught you.

When you pass from this worldly plain, your Perfect Soul, which is actually a very small ball of light, will eventually return to The Lord (for many, this is what is commonly referred to as Heaven). There can be no crap in the presence of The Lord. So how do these tiny balls of light with crap filled filters enter Heaven? There are more stringent filters surrounding Heaven. Only souls in their pure form can return. In order to enter Heaven, the crap has to be filtered out.

Your Perfect Soul uses a blueprint to determine what correct actions and what incorrect actions you have performed in your life. The blueprint goes by the rules The Lord designed. Not the rules you lived by. Not the rules you were taught and for some, not the rules your religion taught you. When you pass on, your Soul in its purest form, not your crap cluttered Spirit controls your fate. It determines what you have done right and done wrong. It determines the reward or punishment you will experience.

Once the reward or punishment have been determined and completed, your spirit can be cleansed and merges with your Perfect Soul & God Gene, forming a new embryo similar to worldly birth and creating a new, Enhanced Soul that can pass through the filter into Heaven. The Perfect Soul becomes the recorder of the life experiences and the cleansed Spirit becomes the memory of the life lived and lessons learned. The God Gene folds into the soul and acts as a direct communication device.

As each soul brings what it has learned from its life experience, that which is God is enriched but the soul that comes to God is not the soul you have lived with, it is the soul you were born with, enriched by your life experience but not tainted by it. God does not evolve, neither does the soul you were born with as they are a constant and evolved far beyond human beings.

Your belief system may play a role and often it plays a great role in the type of reward or punishment you will receive. Bear in mind however, that it will be a Heaven or Hell of your own making. If you believe that Heaven is a place in the clouds populated by Angels and all of your loved ones that is what you will experience when your pure form soul determines you are ready to go there. However, if you believe that Hell is fire and brimstone, you may end up going there at least until your Pure Soul determines that it is time for you to return to The Lord. If, on the other hand, you believe that you will be reincarnated, then that is what will happen to you when your Perfect Soul determines it is time.

So, while you are here, put in the work. Live your life but try and make things better for not only yourself and those you care for but for everyone who is here now and everyone who will be here in the future. The world is at a crossroads. We have within our control, the power to destroy ourselves and this planet. The human race can do this quickly through global nuclear war or slowly through mega pollution. Both of these paths are deadly, one is just quicker than the other. Your actions while you are here help determine the actions of everyone else. Just as your actions will determine your future, the actions of mankind will affect the future of mankind. The journey to Heaven begins with the steps you take today.

12 The Fine Art of Dying

"Dying can be a journey instead of a burden."

Death is an inevitable part of life. Being prepared for it helps both the one dying and the ones who are left behind. Relieving the burden of bills associated with death and burial or cremation is something everyone can do. Some people have jobs with death benefits. Others pay life insurance premiums. Some governments have a social security benefit which taxes working people, puts the money to use and then returns the taxes, with interest, in cash benefits when they retire but sometimes also when they die.

To those who are organized, keep their affairs in order have a will which explains who gets what of their estate have the comfort of knowing that their loved ones are provided for. Those who tell the ones they love how they feel have the comfort of knowing that their loved ones know they were loved. Those who both have their affairs in order and tell their loved ones how they feel can be at peace with the fact that they have not left too many loose ends for their relatives, who know how much they are loved, to clean up.

Those who are generally unorganized, don't have their affairs in order, or don't take the time to tell their loved ones they are loved, can leave this world with many unanswered questions and may have a restless or guilty conscience at the time of their departure.

The manner of death often has its own unique benefits and consequences. Those who die quickly (like in an accident or natural disaster) are spared suffering but they don't have time to set their affairs in order or tell all of their loved ones how they feel. Their loved ones are caught unprepared for their death which can plunge them into despair and chaos, even to the point of disintegrating the family unit. That is where preparing ahead of time comes in handy. It allows you to let your loved ones know how you feel from beyond the grave.

A slow, lingering death (like from disease), are allotted time to set their affairs in order and tell the ones they love how they feel. They also have time to prepare their loved ones for the inevitable. The trade-off is prolonged suffering for both the dying and the loved ones who watch them waste away a little at a time. When those with a prolonged illness die, their loved ones have often been preparing for it. They are sad for their loss but are at peace with the fact that their loved one's suffering has come to an end.

Death, as life is a matter of perception. Those who believe they have lived righteously and who believe there is something for the soul beyond death, leave us ready to partake in the forthcoming adventure. Those who have not lived righteously or who believe in nothingness after life, fear death because they feel that a grand punishment awaits them or that they will simply cease to exist never again enjoying the things they have enjoyed while living.

What happens when you die is what happens. You cannot change it. You can only change the way you experience it through the way you look at it as you are going through the experience. Preparing for death before it happens can help you look at it as less of a burden to yourself and others. Telling those you love that they are loved every day, can reinforce the fact so that if you don't have time to tell them when you go, they already know it, can help ease you conscience. Righting the wrongs you have done in your life, as a continuous practice can help you alleviate future guilt. Acting with compassion and sharing you love with the world can help you to be gone but not forgotten.

13 What Happens When You Die

"There is a trilogy at the beginning of life and at the end of life."

Since the dawn of time, mankind has wondered what happens when we die. Different religions and cultures answer this question differently. Case studies of people who have died and come back arrive at varying conclusions.

Just as the sperm & egg form to create a new organism (the trilogy of procreation) and the building blocks of life, the atom has three parts (proton, neutron and electron, the atomic trilogy) there is a Spiritual Trilogy at the end of life. We are all Perfect Souls. We choose to experience existence as a living being. We call this state of existence life. We begin life as Perfect Souls. Our Perfect Soul has two layers, a protective outer layer known as the Spirit and a protected inner layer, which is the actual Perfect Soul. Both are housed in our body.

The function of your Spirit is to serve as a protective coating for your Perfect Soul that absorbs the things that happen to you in life. The things we experience during our lives act upon us and make impressions upon our Spirit. Over time these impressions surround it and change it. Your Perfect Soul remains within your Spirit as a protected inner layer of spiritual DNA. It does not change and acts as a silent witness to the trials, tribulations, traumas and joys you experience, as well as the good and bad things you do in life. It records all of these things and anything you may have learned from them as a testament to your life.

When you die, the Spiritual Trilogy, your Body, your Spirit and your Perfect Soul do the opposite of what the sperm and egg did at conception. Your Body, which was created at conception, falls away and your Spirit leaves it. What happens to you when you die is determined by your Perfect Soul. Your Perfect Soul is the one The Lord sends you here with. The Soul you are born with is not the Soul you die with. You die with your Perfect Soul intact. It is just inside of your Spirit. Your Spirit is covered up with the crap that is left over from your life experience. The crap that covers your Spirit can include such things as bad decisions you have made, traumas you have not let go of, people and things you don't want to leave, the beliefs and emotions you have held onto. All of these things and more attach themselves to and cover your Spirit, which has served its function, absorbing the shocks your existence has heaped upon you and protected your Perfect Soul. Your Spirit leaves your Body at the time of death. Your Perfect Soul determines when it will conduct you back to The Lord.

Many people are conducted there immediately. Others may have a waiting period. No matter how much crap your beliefs and actions have heaped upon your Spirit, your Perfect Soul knows what to do before you can enter the presence of The Lord. Some People's beliefs and actions may overwhelm them after death causing them to become earth bound spirits. Others may have lived recklessly thinking that they still had time to repent or thought they were fated for hell anyway and might as well enjoy life while they were here, even if their pursuit of joy made others miserable. They may wait for a time in a sort of limbo which humankind has referred to as purgatory or may suffer through several reincarnations but will eventually arrive at their destination.

PSALMS

I'm Beyond Your Perception Of Me
A Song by The Prophet of Life
VERSE 1
It's just the tip of the iceberg you know
You've only scratched the surface
What stands before you is an infinite soul
A life that's filled with purpose
I'm more than
You'll ever know
More than you see

CHORUS
I'm beyond
Your perception
Of me

VERSE 2
You've known me for the longest time
I live and work beside you
You've discounted this heart of mine
Even though it beats true
My love is brighter
Than the stars
Deeper than the sea

CHORUS
I'm beyond

Your perception
Of me

VERSE 3
We walk alone, along the path
Find kindred souls in passing
Learn lessons in the aftermath
Of scars that are everlasting
Life is journey
Of becoming
All we can be
CHORUS
I'm beyond
Your perception
Of me

To Be Loved
A Song by The Prophet of Life

VERSE 1
What a warm feeling it is
To be held
To be touched
To be cared for with tender affection
But most of all to be loved

Once I saw a rich man
Sink to his knees and begin weeping
He built a mighty empire of concrete and steel
But without love, he was nothing

CHORUS
We all want to be loved
I said we all want to be loved
You know, we all want to be loved
To Be Loved
To be loved

VERSE 2
When the night is cold and you are weary
And the burdens that you carry too much

It's a special kind of comfort
To know that you are loved

Soon the problems that you have seem petty
And the shackles around your soul melt away
And the love that you feel surrounds you
And somehow gives you strength

CHORUS
We all want to be loved
I said we all want to be loved
You know, we all want to be loved
To be loved
To be loved

VERSE 3

A rich man can lose his fortune

A man of power can become corrupt

But it's a wise man who knows the secret

Of happiness is to be loved

We all want to be loved
I said we all want to be loved
You know, we all want to be loved
To be loved
To be loved

No Time To Cry
A Song by The Prophet of Life

VERSE 1
Everything's falling apart but I'm not crying
I can always make a brand new start
And keep on trying
Cause bad times they're bound to pass
The trick is to make the good times last

CHORUS
I've got no time to cry
No time to cry
Life's too short
To let it pass by
So I've got no time to cry

VERSE 2
Life isn't always sunshine
There's got to be some rain
But there are always ways of dealing with the pain
Cause bad times they're bound to pass
The trick is to make the good times last

CHORUS
I've got no time to cry

No time to cry
Life's too short
To let it pass by
So I've got no time to cry

Born To Win
A Song by The Prophet of Life

VERSE 1
Nothing can stop you
Once you've got a winning attitude
Put your plan in motion
Get your future on the move

BRIDGE
Go for the glory
Reach out for the top
Set your sights on a goal
And give it all you've got

CHORUS
Born to win
You were born to win
The odds are on your side
Once you begin
You can't lose
Cause you were born to win

VERSE 2
Plough through the roadblocks

That are sitting in your way
With what you've got going
There's no need to be afraid

BRIDGE
Go for the glory
Reach out for the top
Set your sights on a goal
And give it all you've got

CHORUS
Born to win
You were born to win
The odds are on your side
Once you begin
You can't lose
Cause you were born to win

The Gift

A Song by The Prophet of Life

VERSE 1

You keep on trying to find Total happiness Yet time and time again You end up settling for less But the sun comes up each morning So you give it another try While your mind just keeps on wandering To fill the vacuum in your life

CHORUS

The gift is in the thinking

The power in the thoughts you dare

And whenever you need it

The gift will always be there

VERSE 2

Sometimes you are losing Other times you win The difference depends On how you use the gift You keep on searching for answers But questions are all that you get While your mind just keeps on wandering And somehow gives you strength
CHORUS
The gift is in the thinking
The power in the thoughts you dare
And whenever you need it
The gift will always be there

Everybody Makes a Difference
A Song By The Prophet of Life

VERSE 1
Everybody makes a difference
Everyone can be a star
Everybody is important
No matter who or what they are
Everyone can be a hero
We all get a chance to shine
Everybody makes an impact
On their own space and time

VERSE 2
Everybody makes a difference
In everything they do and say
Everyone leaves their mark on humanity
Before they pass away
Everyone has something special
That sets them apart from the pack
That fills a void lying somewhere in this world
Gives strength where strength has lacked

VERSE 3
Everybody makes a difference
All unique but equal
Everybody plays a part in the positive force

That watches over us all
Everybody is a treasure
Everyone is beautiful
Everyone is born in goodness
And there is good in every soul

When the Spirit Moves Me
A Song by The Prophet of Life

VERSE 1
Welcome to my life
Caught up in the pages
Of a nine to five novel
The humming of the computer
The ring of the register
They are my constant companions
Complete with illustrations
Of an endless sea of emotionless faces
Collecting their pay
Counting the days
Until retirement damns them

CHORUS
But when the spirit moves me
When the spirit moves me
I can set myself free
And do great things
Like I know I was meant to
When the spirit moves me
When the spirit moves me
Second chances arise
As dreams come to life
And then they come true

VERSE 2
As the plot develops
I wrestle the anguish
Of a life going nowhere
I watch others pass me by
And feel I'll surely die
At the hands of frustration
But in the end I find
That there is a reason
For my worldly existence
And better things will shine
Once I can find
A way to let them

CHORUS
But when the spirit moves me
When the spirit moves me
I can set myself free
And do great things
Like I know I was meant to
When the spirit moves me
When the spirit moves me
Second chances arise
As dreams come to life
And then they come true

The Best Spiritual Quotes by The Prophet of Life

Preface

I've always liked quotes. Quotes are like little gems of language that say a lot with just a few words. Sometimes they are humorous, other times they are profound. Good quotes can open up worlds of thought and contemplation. They can explain things that one might have previously not been able to comprehend. I particularly like one line quotes that summarize a mood, theme or a concept in one paragraph or less.

This book is filled with quotes I have developed over the past 20 years. My production of quotes really skyrocketed after I began blogging (after 2006), because my writing production increased. As a part of blogging, I have read and commented on other people's blogs. On a website dedicated to my writings by typing the prophet of life ministries into google anywhere in the world, a You Tube site by typing thetureprophetoflife into any you tube search bar and my blog insight by typing insight, the blog of the prophet of life, word press into any google search bar. I have had dialogue with others who have either read, or viewed my writings. All of these things have not only stimulated my writing production, they have created quotes.

Many of the quotes in this book are from blogs, stories and other things I have written. Others are stand-alone quotes which I developed to capture a particular a particular sentiment. Many of my quotes have been used by others including institutions of higher learning, Institutes of medicine, psychologists, scholars, and even recording artists. All of this was done with my written permission of course. I have included quotes on popular topics such as Happiness, Crime and Punishment and Love among others. I have also included some of the places where they have been used. It is my hope that my quotes will open my readers to worlds of thought and inspire and help them understand things at a higher level.

Purchasing this book gives you, as an individuals, a limited license to use any of the quotes in this book for personal use on a non-commercial basis as long as you attribute whatever you use to The Prophet of Life. Use outside of this limited license may be considered copyright infringement and could be punishable to a fine of up to $500.00 per item the copyrighted material appears on and / or in. Uses under this license include such things as using a quote to close an email, on a letter, in a report, or on your website. The proper way to use it is as follows: "Revolution is Evolution" ---The Prophet of Life

Spirituality

The Law of Synchronization

"When your mind, body and spirit are synchronized you are in tune with the ebb and flow of the universe. When you are in tune with the ebb and flow of the universe, you see possibilities that you never noticed before. When you see the new possibilities you create new possibilities. When you create new possibilities that are in tune with the ebb and flow of the universe, you become one with the universe. When you are one with the universe, the universe replies with total acceptance."

"Life is nothing more than a series of experiences. Each person chooses whether of be enlightened by them or to be traumatized by them. I have chosen enlightenment."

"I think one of the challenges in our time just as in times of the past is living spiritually in a material world. Much of the key is attitude and correct attitude can yield perceptual insight. When the mind, body and spirit are in sync, one tends to "notice" the spirituality of everything and in so doing, may realize the ebb and flow of the universe and join in harmony with it."

"It's your life, it's your journey, where you are, is where you want to be."

"When you are at one with the universe, the universe replies with total acceptance."

Mantras utilize the spiritual power of sounds and the teaching power of repetition.
"Freedom is a state of mind. You can be physically in prison yet still be free." ---The Prophet of Life
"The power of life is that each day offers an opportunity to begin again." ---The Prophet of Life

"Self-denial and sacrifice can build character."
"Your perception determines your reality." The Prophet of Life The Prophet of Life from Revelations 2012, The Path of Possibilities, ISBN 978-1-93646200-1
Your soul knows what your ego has yet to perceive.

"Freedom is a state of mind. You can be physically in prison yet still be free."

"There is no such thing as evil. There is however, mental illness."

"Mantras utilize the spiritual power of sounds and the teaching power of repetition."

"The interpretation and experience of both spirituality and religion both depend on the person that is interacting with them. Religion can give one a structure to guide one along their path. Spirituality can also provide a structure but it is a structure that one creates or selects as opposed to one that is pre-made. Religion provides the soundtrack to a spiritual experience but without spirituality, religion has no rhythm. Religion and spirituality are not diametrically opposed. The structure religion provides can be like a body but without spirituality the body cannot have a soul."

"Reality can be perceived when emotion is set aside."

"The concept of the Unity of Prophecy states that all prophets are related in spirit and exist in spirit in the past present and future as a collective. Each prophet takes a turn at incarnation but also provides guidance and support for other prophets who are incarnated when they are not. The message of each prophet delivers is the one that human kind needs at the time of that prophet's incarnation. The messages are in sync with humanities capacity to understand God at that time. The messages of the prophets appear to change because humanities capacity to understand God changes and God delivers further understanding, through the prophets, in increments, over time."

"There are various types of prophecy and there are different kinds of prophets. Some predict the future. Others are given The Word. For most of their lives prophets are not active prophets. They may be prophesying but no one knows them and mostly, no one cares. It takes time for them to build a following. It is all for the best because once they are known, they attract both followers and detractors. They may make powerful friends but also make powerful enemies."

"There is, and always has been a God Business. There is always money in "saving" souls or at least in converting them (and their wallets into your way of thinking). Beyond the monetary considerations, saving souls becomes philosophically important sometimes creating tensions at a fever pitch. Philosophies collide, zealots are created. Wars are waged. Power structures attack perceived competitors to eliminate threats to keeping current followers and attracting new ones. Prophets are often caught in the middle because of the potential threat to the power structure the information they pass on could represent."

"Most Prophets reach a point where they go "High Profile" but they often are killed not long after. It's not easy being a prophet nor is it easy to decide to go "High Profile" because while there may be potential rewards, there are also a plethora of painful / deadly consequences."

"The changed words of the prophets are evolutionary. The original words of the prophets are revolutionary. Both revolution and evolution change the world, one just takes longer than the other. It is true that we have lost the original words of many of the prophets but the original sentiments may yet exist in the altered versions. The word is clarified by prophets and those who come after them. The Lord always sends prophets to continue to clarify humankind's understanding of The Word. Prophets are like Doritos. The Lord keeps making more."

"Religion gives people a structure to build their lives and their worship around."

"We are all born with an original soul. As we proceed down the path of our life, we accumulate things, traumas, pleasures, beliefs (including religious) and habits through our experience and education. All of these things cover over our original soul to form what we call our spirit. Our spirit is our original soul with all of the "baggage" we have accumulated through our life."

"Jesus taught us many things. But so did Muhammad and Buddha and countless others. You don't need priests or prophets to teach you. People and events in your life can teach you."

"Your path is like a mystery that unfolds as we travel it. The journey itself is half the fun!"
"Life is a journey your soul chose to take. The world is meant to be our school. We are all here to learn the lessons that life has to teach us and return with that knowledge to God. What we learn not only enriches our soul but every soul in the universe. In this way, every living being, no matter how short their life, learns something and contributes something to the whole."

"All souls have existed since the beginning of time and will exist until the end of time. It is only when they are residing with and totally bonded with the collective in heaven that they have an understanding memory of the past-present-future that we know as eternal time. They have this understanding memory on a non-linear level. This understanding memory is rarely reached on a conscious level for souls that are going through an incarnation although many can receive glimpses of it during an incarnation on a subconscious level."

"Reality can be perceived when emotion is set aside."

"Think of it as your original soul is your operating system and your spirit consists of various software programs you acquire on your journey. Your original soul is, for the most part running silently in the background while you load various software programs to help you decipher and react to what is happening in your life. Your original soul has a backup which records everything that you experience and what you learned from it (if anything)."

"The power of THE WORD it sneaks up on you so subtly you think it's telling you something you've known all along."

"There are streams of consciousness in the universe. When someone invents something or creates something, often someone else invents or creates something similar and often at the same or nearly the same time. I believe that when the universe needs something, a desire is instilled to discover, invent or create it. If one person who is called upon to do the actual discovering, inventing."

"When you die, your original soul takes over and ejects your software. It returns to God who then deciphers the backup and is thus enriched by it. Sometimes the software refuses to leave the operating system which leaves it stuck on earth until it is separated.
In this case, you have a ghost."

"The interpretation and experience of spirituality and religion both depend on the person that is interacting with them."

"When humanity looks at ourselves without labels and just as great spirits, we will shed the "isms" (sexism, racism, etc.) and the persecutions that come with them."

"There are two types of dimensions. Those we perceive and those we do not. Those we do not include the spiritual dimension."

"Your soul knows what your ego has yet to perceive."

"Spirituality, in essence is an individual enterprise, whether one is engaged in a religious community or not. We are all on our own journey, no matter what beliefs or ideals we may attach ourselves to on our path."

"Enlightenment is a very personal endeavor. One can become enlightened daily in small ways, every now and then one gets an "AHA" moment and once in a while a revelation. This short write up seems to preview a book about conclusions derived from someone's personal experience. That's actually what most literature is about, living vicariously and growing from insights gained from other's experience."

Jesus taught us many things. But so did Muhammad and Buddha Krishna, Moses and countless others. You don't need priests or prophets to teach you. People and events in your life can teach you.

Just as there is some darkness in every soul, there is some light in every soul.

Souls do not need to be saved. Egos need clarification.

"I think that I have always been able to see things both from within myself and outside of

myself simultaneously. This has, I believe been one of my saving graces."

"Spirituality is like a game. The game is constantly changing and regenerating. It is simultaneously being played by everyone and by one individual. You as an individual play the game amidst billions of others but despite distractions that present themselves. The only important player to you is you."

"We each walk our own path. All paths lead to the same destination but different beings arrive at it at different times. Each path is like a mystery that unfolds as we travel it. The journey itself is half the fun!"

Although many people define their spiritualism through a religion, you don't have to be religious to be spiritual.

Our physical bodies, though powerful are merely facades. They are clothing for our spirit.

Your true spiritual nature is to trust. Your true spiritual nature is to respect. Your true spiritual nature is to love unconditionally.

"Every spiritual journey begins with baby steps and evolves into long strides. The most profound revelations occur in the baby steps, and the high that is created often inspires and propels the rest of the journey."

"Humility is meant to keep one from getting a swelled head. Obedience is meant to give one structure and discipline. When combined with purpose, whether that purpose is religious, job related or furthering one's education, humility and obedience can equal success."

"Your perception determines your reality. Change your perception and you change your reality."

"Many of us search for the answers, but in truth they are all around us. We don't always know how to home in on them."

"Religion isn't a prerequisite to finding God. Religion is merely a path but there are many paths. Some may try to tell you that their way is the only way but that is more a device created by people who want to attract and keep followers to a religion than an actual fact."

We all travel in two worlds, the human world and spirit world, with friends from both sides assisting us with our life's journey.

Let the light that is within me illuminate humanity.

"Your true spiritual nature is to trust. Your true spiritual nature is to respect. Your true spiritual nature is to love unconditionally. As you go through your life, however, things happen to you and you develop an ego as a reaction of the things that happen to you. People take advantage of your trust and you learn to trust a little less. While respect is natural, disrespect is also learned. Your loving heart is repeatedly broken and love is no longer unconditional. Is it any wonder that people develop prejudices and hatreds for those who are different? Is it any wonder that religions fight against each other to obtain or defend spiritual conquests? Is it any wonder that nations should declare war, genocide and ethnic cleansing upon each other?"

"The original Bible was the Word of God as interpreted by men but as it has been changed, altered and translated it has become more a version of the Word of God as interpreted by men of religion who often had an agenda that was based on the current needs of their religion."

"The interpretation and experience of both spirituality and religion both depend on the person that is interacting with them. Religion can give one a structure to guide one along their path. Spirituality can also provide a structure but it is a structure that one creates or selects as opposed to one that is pre-made. Religion provides the soundtrack to a spiritual experience but without spirituality, religion has no rhythm. Religion and spirituality are not diametrically opposed. The structure religion provides can be like a body but without spirituality the body cannot have a soul."

"Reality can be perceived when emotion is set aside."

"The concept of the Unity of Prophecy states that all prophets are related in spirit and exist in spirit in the past present and future as a collective. Each prophet takes a turn at incarnation but also provides guidance and support for other prophets who are incarnated when they are not. The message of each prophet delivers is the one that human kind needs at the time of that prophet's incarnation. The messages are in sync with humanities capacity to understand God at that time. The messages of the prophets appear to change because humanities capacity to understand

God changes and God delivers further understanding, through the prophets, in increments, over time."

"We each walk our own path. All paths lead to the same destination but different beings arrive at it at different times. Each path is like a mystery that unfolds as we travel it. The journey itself is half the fun!"

"Religion is not God. It is merely humankind's attempt to understand God."

"Many of us search for the answers, but in truth they are all around us. We don't always know how to home in on them. Religion isn't a prerequisite to finding God. Religion is merely a path but there are many paths. Some may try to tell you that their way is the only way but that is more a device created by people who want to attract and keep followers to a religion than an actual fact."

"What I have come to realize regarding this topic is as follows: we are all born with an original soul. As we proceed down the path of our life, we accumulate things, traumas, pleasures, beliefs (including religious) and habits through our experience and education. All of these things cover over our original soul to form what we call our spirit. Our spirit is our original soul with all of the "baggage" we have accumulated through our life."

"Think of it as your original soul is your operating system and your spirit consists of various software programs you acquire on your journey. Your original soul is, for the most part running silently in the background while you load various software programs to help you decipher and react to what is happening in your life. Your original soul has a backup which records everything that you experience and what you learned from it (if anything)."

"When you die, your original soul takes over and ejects your software. It returns to God who then deciphers the backup and is thus enriched by it. Sometimes the software refuses to leave the operating system which leaves it stuck on earth until it is separated. Other times, the software is left by itself on this worldly plane and repeats over and over like a glitch or a recording that plays continuously at certain intervals. In either of these cases, you have a ghost."

"What religion you are doesn't matter. You don't even have to have a religion to come to The Lord. Everyone comes to The Lord eventually, even atheists."

"The universe talks to all of us. We just need to know how to listen."

"Whatever you believe Christ was, great man, prophet or God, you can take comfort knowing that whatever Christ was to you, he chose to live as you do. He went through the same struggles that you do. In this, you are one with Christ and through you, Christ lives."

"Enlightenment can happen to anyone who is open to it. You don't have to be chosen, you merely have to choose to be open to it."

"We all take our own spiritual journey. A particular religion can be part of that but doesn't have to be. Many, grow beyond their religions but many in the world don't."

"We all walk a path in our life experience. If we are diligent and lucky, we receive and interpret the signs that are given to us correctly we find the path that we were meant to be on instead of taking a wrong turn and ending up on the wrong path."

"When me go with my ego then I can't grow."

"You are here for a purpose. There's more to you than can be seen from the surface."

"If everyone fell in love with someone from a group they hate the most, there would no longer be hatred in the world. They would either give in to that love or destroy themselves for feeling it."

"We are all on separate paths. We may have others on our path with us from time to time, but we journey as individuals."

"Religion gives people a structure to build their lives and their worship around."

"Your body is merely an extension of your soul. Disease is meant to discomfort you, not kill you. Love is meant to heal you. Life is meant to teach you."

"When you do good things, good things come back to you. To put it more simply, when you do good you get good."

"Money and power are fleeting. They are merely illusions that can lead to delusions of grandeur and the false belief that one is not susceptible to the fragility of human life."

"One of life's greatest challenges is to live spiritually in a material world. Living spiritually can be done through a religion and many do this but religion is more than going to a place of worship, it is taking the place of worship with you, wherever you go. Living spiritually is a matter of perception if you perceive the world spiritually, you notice the spirituality in everything."

"My faith teaches me a completely different view of Karma. There may be some Karma at play, for instance if the multiple death incident involves a super storm that is the result of global warming and all of those people have, in past and current life done things that contribute to global warming then it could play a part in it. However, many of the tragic events that occur are either due to the negligence of humankind or natural forces like earthquakes and storms. If you live on a fault line is it karma that caused you to die in an earthquake or your own ignorance (you didn't know you live on a fault line) or stubbornness, (you bought there because it cost you less money and now you can't afford to move). The purpose of life is to teach lessons. Natural forces occur not because God makes them happen to particular people, they happen because that is the system that God set up for this planet. Who they happen to is often a matter of personal choice in the life you have now. Both the person who survives a disaster and the person who succumbs to it learn a lesson the difference is the one who survives gets to tell his friends and relatives and by sharing it, offers them a chance to learn from it as well. "Some people learn from their mistakes and others avoid making mistakes by learning from the mistakes of others." ---The Prophet of Life

Mercy

"Authentic mercy is taking extenuating circumstances into account when administering justice. It is looking at the perpetrator as a salvageable human being instead of a monster to be punished into submission."

"To show kindness and mercy to others, especially strangers is an act that bestows the blessings of The Lord on both the giver and receiver."

Life Lessons

"Some people learn from their mistakes. Others avoid making mistakes by learning from the mistakes of others."

"Wherever you are in life is a result of the choices you made and actions you took or did not take."

"Decisions made in anger can yield a lifetime of regret."

"Our lives are filled with doorways. Each one can lead to a new adventure."

"Many things peak and wane in your life. Much of life (and time) is filled with streams of consciousness that circulate and re-circulate. Humanity is growing and changing and evolving and so are you."

"What is needed is in the world is mutual respect and the realization that not everyone in the world believes as you do but if you respect them, you agree to disagree."

"Hindsight is 20/20. Research. Plan. Execute. Evaluate. This makes your forward vision 20/20."

"Enlightenment can happen to anyone who is open to it. You don't have to be chosen, you merely have to choose to be open to it."

"Self denial and sacrifice build character."

"It is a good thing for one to be fulfilled within oneself but it is the people who are not fulfilled that change the world, while seeking fulfillment."

"Wherever you are in life is a result of the choices you made and actions you took or did not take."

"Leadership is a collaborative endeavor."

"Life teaches us that ignoring a problem won't make it go away, instead, it allows it to grow into a bigger problem."

"Self-confidence often comes from familiarity through experience. In athletes it comes from practice, in scholars it comes from study. Often, the more familiar you are with something, the more confident you become. This is because there aren't any unknowns or at least they are minimized. It is fear of the unknown that holds many people back. The experiential familiarity that comes from practice or study eliminates and / or minimizes the unknown."

"Life can be your greatest teacher once you are open to learning from experience."

"My life is a never ending series of miracles. Yours can be too if you take time to notice the miracles around you."

"People tend to remember the good more than the bad, the victories more than the struggles that gave birth to them."

"Mantras utilize the spiritual power of sounds and the teaching power of repetition."

"Your life is a never ending lesson."

"Your body is merely an extension of your soul. Disease is meant to discomfort you, not kill you. Love is meant to heal you. Life is meant to teach you."

"When me go with my ego then me can't grow."

"No life is useless. Every life has a purpose. Even those which you think have no purpose. The purpose is just beyond your frame of reference."
"Change does not occur as the result of a few great men making momentous decisions. Change occurs as a result of small actions by a large group of people simultaneously."

It is a good thing for one to be fulfilled within oneself but it is the people who are not fulfilled that change the world, while seeking fulfillment."

"Growing up is not growing old."
"Self-denial and sacrifice build character."

"Part of the reason of your existence is to learn what this existence teaches you. The lesson never ends. Things that you see, stories you hear, things that happen to others that you know and things that happen to you are all potential lessons. They may not be lessons for your use in the immediate future (although many times you are warned about something several times before it actually occurs), but it will come in handy at some point."

"When your mind, body and spirit are synchronized you are in tune with the ebb and flow of the universe. When you are in tune with the ebb and flow of the universe, you see possibilities that you never noticed before. When you see the new possibilities you act to create new possibilities. When you create new possibilities that are in tune with the ebb and flow of the universe, you become one with the universe. When you are one with the universe, the universe replies with total acceptance."

"In reality, what you do about anything doesn't matter to God, as you have free will. It matters to you. Deep in your spiritual DNA, you know what is right and what is wrong. It is natural to do the right thing, natural but not always easy. If Karma gets you, it's not because God sent Karma to get you, it is because you sent Karma to get you."

"Those who cease to grow, cease to live."
"Hope is born with each new day."
"Growing up is not growing old."

"The point of racism is to dehumanize those targeted by the racism. Violence as a reaction to injustice provides ammunition to racists."

From the book "Black in America" by The Prophet of Life

"Prejudice is not a symptom of stupidity. Nor is it a symptom of evil. It is merely a symptom of ignorance."

"Many are so caught up in their own problems that they cannot see the big picture. Often, seeing the big picture can give one the perspective that makes illusive solutions suddenly easy to visualize. One form of hope can be accessed through stepping outside of yourself and seeing the bigger picture."

Suffering is in the grand scheme of things. It is meant to teach a lesson. Sometimes it takes a lot of repeating until the lesson is learned. Both good and bad people reap the benefits of the sunshine. Both good and bad people receive rain for their crops. Chaos and disaster befalls both the good and the bad. The difference in the aftermath of tragedy is the lesson learned or not learned.

"Just something to think about...Life is a learning experience and one can choose to reincarnate or not. Life is a journey your soul chose to take. There are still souls who have not chosen to take the journey. Also, when you look beyond this planet and consider that reincarnation doesn't have to be on this planet but can be on another as another type of life form, you can begin to see the bigger picture. Humanity only has about 137 pieces of a thousand piece puzzle. There is still much to be revealed."

"Many things peak and wane in your life. Much of life (and time) is filled with streams of consciousness that circulate and re-circulate. Humanity is growing and changing and evolving and so are you."

"Reality is wrapped within a fantasy when your life is interpreted by your ego."

"The power of life is that each day offers an opportunity to begin again."

"Animals have a way of sensing your true nature and often respond accordingly."

"Obstacles are merely lessons that can lead to success."

"We are taught the religion or life philosophy of the culture we grow up in but we are expected to grow beyond it There's a lot out in the world and what you have grown to know may be right for you but how will you really know unless you see what else is out there? Even if nothing out there is satisfying to you, you can gain insights into different peoples and cultures that will broaden your understanding of people in general. Traveling also can expose you to different cultures and new ideas which in turn, will broaden your understanding of humanity and life on our planet."

Life is a journey. You may be at a fork in the road but it is the forks in the road that make life interesting and lead us to new adventures.

Life teaches us that ignoring a problem won't make it go away, instead, it allows it to grow into a bigger problem.

"Enlightenment can happen to anyone who is open to it. You don't have to be chosen, you merely have to choose to be open to it."

"Self confidence often comes from familiarity through experience. In athletes it comes from practice, in scholars it comes from study. Often, the more familiar you are with something, the more confident you become. This is because there aren't any unknowns or at least they are minimized. It is fear of the unknown that holds many people back. The experiential familiarity that comes from practice or study eliminates and / or minimizes the unknown."

Life

"There are few things one can count on in life. Problems and the need to change are two of them" The Prophet of Life from Revelations 2012, The Path of Possibilities, ISBN 978-1-93646200-
"A person whose mind and spirit are free can never be oppressed."

"Life is a journey your soul chose to take."
"Life is a test you cannot afford to fail."

"Life is a learning experience."
"Life is a learning experience and every experience is a lesson."

"I have a Masters in Life Degree from The College of The Streets."

"The power of life is that each day offers an opportunity to begin again."

Life presents us with many doorways. Some doorways appear to hold us back but when we look back at the experience from the vantage point of the future, we find that they actually moved us forward."

"In life, sometimes you have a maid and sometimes you are a maid."

"In life, as in acting, sometimes you play an extra in the background of a scene, other times you get the leading role."

Life is change. Master change and you can master life.

Life is a struggle but it beats the alternative.

"Those who cease to grow, cease to live."

"Every life is precious. Every life is important. Every life has a purpose."

"Money and power are fleeting. They are merely illusions that can lead to delusions of grandeur and the false belief that one is not susceptible to the fragility of human life."

"I cannot tell you what happens when you die. I can only tell you what happened to me."

"I cannot tell you what it is like to communicate with God. I can only tell you how God communicates with me. My life has been filled with miracles and obstacles. I have known wonderful pleasures and jaw dropping horrors. For years, I was saddled with storms of my own creation but I have made it through them. I have had a rich tapestry of experiences. Your experiences may be entirely different."

"Life can be your greatest teacher once you are open to learning from experience."

"My life is a never ending series of miracles. Yours can be too if you take time to notice the miracles around you."

Knowledge

"Knowledge is power, those who increase knowledge increase empowerment."

"I have a Masters in Life Degree from The College of The Streets."

"I am not better than you. I am merely better informed."

Inspirational

"Imagination is the jet fuel that uplifts humanity."
"Those who have done the impossible often didn't know it was impossible when they did it."
The Prophet of Life Memorial Tribute to Steve Jobs, You Tube Video

Everybody makes a difference.

When your world is collapsing all around you, it is time to reinvent yourself.

"Leadership is a collaborative endeavor."
"Of all the souls who have ever lived, you have been chosen to live in these times." 2012 New Years Message you tube video
"When your life is a constant series of miracles, every moment becomes your greatest moment, until the next one happens."

"The world is changed by simple ideas put into practice." The Prophet of Life
from: Revelations of 2012, The Path of Possibilities
ISBN # 978-1-93646200-1
"A new day is dawning there is a revolution in the psyche of humanity." The Prophet of Life
from: Revelations of 2012, The Path of Possibilities
ISBN # 978-1-93646200-1

"Persistence can melt away resistance."

"Incremental planning and sustained execution can make the insurmountable possible."

"Courage is the ability to act in spite of fear."
"Failure is not truly failure unless you fail to learn from it."
"Work can turn dreams into reality."
"Planning can make dreams into reality."
"Having a goal can make dreams into reality."
"Incremental planning and sustained execution can make the insurmountable possible."
The balance of mind, body and spirit is the key to preventing and curing disease.

We can work together as one race, the human race to heal the planet, heal the food chain and heal ourselves in the process. The time for selfish thinking is over. The time for thinking globally and acting locally is in the middle of its tenure. The time for thinking and acting cooperatively is about to dawn.

The solution to our problems does not lie in the knowledge and resources of any one culture or nation but in the knowledge and resources of all of them, both ancient and modern. We have the power to determine our future. Our actions today will determine our benefits or consequences tomorrow. Be it feast or famine, the future shall be a heaven or hell of our own making.

"Even the poorest among us deserve the dignity of equality." The Prophet of Life

From Inspirational Quotes by The prophet of Life You Tube video

Miracles are vision that supersedes reality.

Miracles happen when vision supersedes reality. Positive motivation is the life force of an enlightened generation

The attitude of "Yes I Can" works best when you've got a plan.

Every life is precious. Every life is important. Every life has a purpose.

"No Matter what language you speak, Mother Is spelled LOVE
Where would you be without your mother? You would not be here."

From the book "True Stories of Inspiration and General Interest" by The Prophet of Life

Humanity

"It takes all kinds of people to make the human race and everyone fits in their own way."
"Humanity is a work in progress."
"A new day is dawning there is a revolution in the psyche of humanity."

"We are all unique and all have a unique world view and definition of reality."

"Everybody makes a difference."
"It takes all kinds of people to make the human race and everyone fits in their own way."

"For humanity to uniformly experience a more positive reality we must first collectively (it shall begin one person at a time) believe that a better world is possible and then work towards it. Then our perceptions will change and with it, our reality."

"We are not capitalist. We are not communist. We are humanist." From A New Revolution
from: Revelations of 2012, The Path of Possibilities
ISBN # 978-1-93646200-1

"Humanity is currently changing from puberty into adulthood."
"The age of childish beliefs and actions is coming to an end. The time to face up to adult responsibilities is coming into fruition."

"We, as a human race, should move away from stereotypes and towards a brighter future together, as equals."
"Since everyone is worthy of God's love, no one is worthless."

It is a good thing for one to be fulfilled within oneself but it is the people who are not fulfilled that change the world, while seeking fulfillment."

 It takes all kinds of people to make the human race and everyone fits in their own way.

God has never said and neither the Major Prophets that women are inferior to men. Old time views of life and the male dominated religions that sprang out of them propagated the notion that women are inferior to men. In fact, feminism is the next logical step in the natural progression of humanity. As I believe that the things written in Revelations of 2012 are God's plan for humanity for the next millennium, I believe with all of my heart that women are equal to men and that global liberation of women and elevation to the status of equals to men shall take place

Let the light that's within me shine through this city and illuminate every soul within its walls. Let a positive vision conquer superstition and rise as a blessing to us all.

Declare peace. It is time to heal all things war's torn to shreds. Declare peace. We shall not take stock in violence ever again.   From Declare Peace

So much suffering and heartache Bourne upon this worldly plain, so many caught up in it that can't see beyond their pain. Cries the wisdom of the ages all wounds are healed in time. Like a beacon to the future shines the inspiration that Hope is the answer. From Finding God in A Chaotic World, a part of the Revelations of 2012 Beyond Faith series.

Life holds no guarantees because the world is made up of people and people don't come with guarantees,

I don't want to own you. Don't want to control you. I just want to be good to you. From the song I Just Wanna Be Good To You

In times of desperation inner communication brings forth an understanding light. From the song One World, One People

The pain stings like an open wound. Rub in salt and only bitterness blooms. Get at the root of the feeling and a wisdom is born that starts the healing. We Keep Hurting Each Other From The Play Jesus

Humanity shall not realize its potential until all members of the human family make a unilateral decision to abolish war.

"Even the poorest among us deserve the dignity of equality," ¬The Prophet of Life From the book: Revelations of 2012 ISBN# 978-1-93646200-1

"The solution to our problems does not lie in the knowledge and resources of any one culture or nation but in the knowledge and resources of all of them, both ancient and modern

"We have the power to determine our future. Our actions today will determine our benefits or consequences tomorrow."

"A new day is dawning there is a revolution in the psyche of humanity."

"The time for selfish thinking is over. The time for thinking globally and acting locally is in the middle of its tenure. The time for thinking and acting cooperatively is about to dawn."

"Humanity shall not realize its potential until all members of the human family make a unilateral decision to abolish war."

"It takes all kinds of people to make the human race and everyone fits in their own way."

"Pride through true equality is what the world needs."

"I cry for humanity because humanity is too self-absorbed to cry for itself."

One world, one people two sexes both equal, twelve billion eyes, six billion souls see through them, but just one race and that is human. From the Song One World, One People

"Humanity is a work in progress."

Heaven & Hell

"In the human experience, one person's hell is another person's existence."

"The entrance to Heaven is restricted. There are filters surrounding heaven. Only pure spirits can enter. The filters pull the crap out of any spirit attempting to enter. For most people whose spirits attempt to enter heaven the filters pull out the baggage from your incarnation. All that enters is the part of your soul that records what you did during your life along with memories and the knowledge gained from the experience."

"Hell is a matter of perception."

"Heaven exists. It is a physical location but it exists in another dimension, a dimension only accessible by spirits. Heaven is a collective of souls that are not currently incarnated. Heaven holds souls from the past and souls from this planet and all souls past, present and future from everywhere that exists, has existed and will exist in the future. Heaven is made up entirely of energy. This is because all souls are made up of energy. A soul can be described as a small ball of energy which can manifest itself as a small ball of light. The cumulative collective of all of these souls illuminates the universe."

"The heaven you expect is the heaven you get."

"The experience of heaven itself is a matter of perception and is perceived differently by the souls that are there depending on the state of their elevation to the truth. To those who first return from an incarnation it may be perceived as a place where their loved ones are awaiting them. This is because many souls returning from an incarnation still cling to vestiges of their ego. After a period of time however, the need for connection to souls you were incarnated with gives way to the higher purpose of bonding with the entire collective. This is where souls really begin to understand the answers to the type of deep existence questions that humanity has been asking since its beginnings."

"Hell is a never ending itch with no salve to heal it and no appendages to scratch it."

"Heaven is more than a state of mind."

"Even the most impure spirits have a "Pure Soul" that records their experience and knowledge but with impure spirits, any impure knowledge or experiences are erased. Impure spirits can begin to enter heaven but the surrounding filters pull out so much of the crap that has become their "Identity" that they are rendered something completely different from what they came to know of themselves. A very painful and irreversible experience for any impure spirit, but a very necessary one because impurities cannot exist in the place where The Lord Dwells."

God resides everywhere but spirits reside in a collective which many religions call heaven. The Godforce is strong in that place which is in a different dimension. That which many consider evil cannot enter there and the bad that is in souls after each life falls away before the soul can enter. The traditional heaven where you see your friends and family and pets is a transitional area to help ease the trauma of transitioning from life to a completely spiritual existence. Hell, is also a transitional place where souls can do penance but it is chosen by the soul itself not by God. Many think Karma is delved out by God or by universal forces but it is actually delved out by your own inner soul which is different from your outer soul. --- Revelations of 2012

God

For more extensive quotes about god see the Kindle book Quotes about God by The prophet of Life.

"Humanity trying to comprehend the nature of God is like an ant trying to comprehend a forest the size of North America."

"People often wonder why God allows hunger, poverty and war in our world. Perhaps God wonders why we allow it."

"To save a life, any life, be it animal, vegetable or human is an act on behalf of The Lord."

"For God so loves all of life that all of life is endowed with a part of The Lord in their spiritual DNA."
The Prophet of Life from Revelations of 2012, The Path of Possibilities, ISBN# 978-1-93646200-1

"It is only God that exists in the past, present and future simultaneously. We have only the present."

"Everything is part of God's plan. Even the people and things they do that seem to go against God."

"The Lord is not ever changing, humanity's ability to understand that which is The Lord evolves in increments over long periods of time."
From **The Tenants of Revelations of 2012**

"God is justice, God is compassion. God is beyond all things that you can imagine. God is love."
From the song God Is Love by The Prophet of Life

"God is not a religion. Religion is humanity trying to understand God."

"Since everyone is worthy of God's love, no one is worthless."

"Those who perform an act of kindness have the power to bestow the blessings of The Lord. The blessing is bestowed upon both the giver and the receiver.

Fear

"Fear can be like a prison. It is, however, a self made prison. Many are imprisoned by fear. No one else can liberate them from this prison. Others may inspire them but they must liberate themselves."

"Fear is the purgatory of unimaginative minds."

"To defeat a bully, you must take all aspects of control away from him."

Faith

"What is the difference between a believer and someone who has faith? A believer is one who will take a step into the unknown because he or she believes that God will protect them from harm. A person of faith will take a step into the unknown not knowing whether or not they will be protected from harm but knowing that it is God's will that they must do so and therefore, harm is not an important issue."

"Faith cannot protect you from disaster it can help you recover from it."

"True Faith Does not need miracles or wish fulfillment to sustain itself.

"True Faith Does not need miracles or wish fulfillment to sustain itself. The Lord is not your fairy godmother."

"I don't try and change anyone's faith or convert them to my way of thinking. I merely offer information from a perspective they may no have considered."

"Difficult times are meant to test one's character and perhaps even one's faith."

"I may lose faith in myself from time to time but I have never lost faith in The Lord."

"I have always had faith but my faith has deepened as my life progressed."

Natural disasters are part of the workings of the universe and not a punishment from God upon a particular community. Prayer is not meant to yield a miracle that saves you from suffering and disaster, what is meant to happen will happen. Prayer and faith help you deal with it. Many people feel that there is no God after they have suffered but faith helps you through suffering it doesn't prevent it, so they falsely blame God because their ego tells them god should have prevented the disaster or suffering from happening to them. --- The Prophet of Life

There may be some Karma at play, if for example, the disaster is a result of global warming and each person has in past lives and their current life contributed to it. However, many disasters occur due to the negligence of humankind or natural forces. The natural forces do not occur because God is out to get particular group of people. The natural forces occur because that is how God set up the system on this planet. The purpose of life is to teach lessons. Both the person who survives and the one who does not learn a lesson from the experience. The difference is the one who is alive can tell their friends and relatives the lesson they learned and by doing so can give them the gift of allowing them to learn from another's mistake instead of having to make the mistake themselves. ---The Prophet of Life

"Faith is walking a path through the darkness, not knowing where the obstacles are, where the path will lead you but walking, down the path, through the darkness, anyway."

"I find the notion of faith as a protection from suffering or pain particularly interesting. Faith is beyond pain & suffering. People often look at faith from their own point of view instead of The Lord's. People often pray for things that they want with some expectation of wish fulfillment. The Lord is not your fairy godmother. True faith does not depend on wish fulfillment or miracles to sustain itself."

How Believing Can Change The World

"Belief is a powerful thing. Belief is what motivates humanity to do almost everything good and bad. It is belief that has helped create everything ever invented, Belief helps determine perception and your perception determines your reality. A concept that begins with one person, can, through communication, spread to tens, hundreds, thousands, millions and even billions of others. For humanity to uniformly experience a more positive reality we must first collectively believe that a better world is possible and then work towards it. Then our perceptions will change and with it, our reality."

Death

"Death can be a rewarding experience spiritually. You are given many pieces of your personal puzzle and many questions raised on your life journey are answered."

"When I died, I became a ball of pure light."

"My death experience was different from most, but then again I was way younger than most when it happened. It took me years to figure out what it meant and then only through dreams and other communications."

My Death

"I was very young about two when I died. I went into convulsions and my grandmother saw this and had a heart attack. When the paramedics came they pronounced me dead and went to work on my grandmother. Several minutes later, a doctor passing by saw the ambulance & went inside to see what was happening. I don't know why he did that but I suppose one of my spiritual guides guided him there. He entered and the paramedics told him they were working on Granny & I was dead. The doctor then revived me (probably manually I don't believe those electroshock machines were around in the 1950's). I was then in a coma packed in ice for 8 weeks."

"My death experience was vivid but as a child I didn't understand any of it. I didn't understand why there was a light shining through the ceiling in my dark room when I was very little or why I met people who called themselves angels or why people I knew came to me when they died or why ghosts would seek me out and why they would follow my directions. When I was in my late teens I had a series of dreams that replayed my death experience but in slow motion. This revealed a lot of nuances that had been missing previously. The nuances made the difference."

"We all die. Death is a part of life as natural as breathing."

"No one ever really dies, we just change levels of understanding."

"The Path of our life experience continues beyond death and all that is gained through life experience is returned to The Lord."

"My death experience was different than others I have heard of. I was not in a dark tunnel with a light at the end of it. I was a small ball of light going through outer space towards what looked like the Milky Way, at a high rate of speed. As I moved towards the star cluster, other balls of light flew past me in an opposite direction making whooshing sounds as they passed. When I was brought back to life, I was in a coma for eight weeks. I revisited this time through a series of dreams, over a period of years. I came to see it in slow motion and when slowed down, the balls of light that passed me were saying things to me. Some of these things have been the basis of part of my writings."

"He's a businessman, he's international. Pick your poison he's got them all. A gun to solve your problem, a drug to ease your pain, child labor or bloodstained clothing, nuclear rain. From Death is Driving A Cadillac a song by Teacherz. Lyrics by the Prophet of Life

"He's cruising up your street, looking for souls to take. Misery is by his side, destruction in his wake. He rides the needle tracks of your soul, the scars of greed and lust. Flesh and blood melt before him, dreams turn into dust." From Death is driving A Cadillac a song by Teacherz. Lyrics by the Prophet of Life

"In the place where I went when I died, there were all souls but when I returned to the same body, I returned with a different understanding of clarity than most of the living do not have. Not a better clarity, because, in reality, there is no better or worse, just a different clarity. When I was there, time stood still and moments were stretched beyond our understanding of time. Now, for me, there is a doorway between the living and the dead. The dead know me and know of me. They are both attracted and repelled by me because they do not understand how someone can register as dead like them, yet be of flesh in the material world. I understand, because it is my journey. Everyone's journey is different, and whether you believe it or not, everyone's life has a purpose which ultimately enriches that which is God."

Revelations of 2012

Finding God in a Chaotic World

Chapters 1-11 & Psalms

Preface

The world can seem very chaotic these days. Humankind is constantly changing, and evolving. Advances in science have made it possible to travel thousands of miles in a matter of hours. We can keep in touch with people we care about and even with the world at large with the push of a button. Many of the diseases that have plagued humankind for centuries have been wiped out. Yet there is still poverty. There is still famine. There is still disease. There is still war. There is still injustice.

Billions of people desire to become closer to God. They gravitate towards established religions or towards spirituality but still, feel unfulfilled. They have so many questions that remain unanswered. They pray, they talk to religious leaders, they talk with other people but still never find the answers. They want to talk to God but don't know how.

Others feel they are out of touch with God. They have become unsure if God even exists. They don't see any evidence of God at work in their world or in their personal lives. They can't find solace in established religion but don't know how to find God on their own.

Still others know the end is near. They see the signs everywhere. They point to every natural disaster, every war, every famine, every new disease that is discovered and every bad thing done to and by humanity, as evidence. They are waiting for God to come out of the sky and rescue their group and send everyone else to hell.

The end is not near. The end is not here. What the world is experiencing is not the end of days but a transitional period. Humanity is experiencing growing pains. And just like other times when humanity was in a transitional period, God has sent a messenger with information to help guide humanity through this period.

God does exist. God is at work in our world. God is at work in all of our lives. God communicates with humanity and God communicates with you. Didn't you get the messages God has been sending you your whole life? Some who utter that phrase will tell you the message is in a particular scripture and then try to convert you. That is not what I am talking about here. God communicates with you. God sends personal messages to you. They are usually not in writing.

Many will tell you "The Lord works in mysterious ways." What they are really telling you is they don't know the answer. The Lord does not work in mysterious ways. There is a purpose and beauty in all that God does and although many don't notice it, it is there for those who know what to look for.

This book tells you how The Lord communicates with you. This book will teach you a lot of new things about God. Things you may have never heard before but things that will somehow make sense. If you learn the lesson that this book is meant to teach, you will begin to see the world differently. You will begin to see your life differently. You will see the purpose in some of the things you have always thought were purposeless. This book is not an attempt to convert you to a new religion. Whatever religion you are currently is okay as long as it works for you.

This book will give you a different way of looking at God. The knowledge within these pages can restore your faith. It can lighten your burden. It can show you the God I have come to know, a God that doesn't bark orders but makes suggestions. A God that isn't jealous or vain. A God that doesn't punish but teaches lessons. If you want to know that God I invite you to read on.

Chapter One
The Nature of The Lord

"For The Lord so loves all of life, that all living beings are endowed with a part of The Lord."

Everyone whether they realize it or not, believes in a higher power. Different philosophies have different names for this higher power. I call this higher power The Lord. The sum total of mankind's knowledge of The Lord probably consists of 137 pieces of a thousand piece puzzle. The essence of The Lord does not change, mankind's perception of The Lord does. The human race has come to a greater understanding of themselves and The Lord in increments over long periods of time.

The Lord exists in the past present and future simultaneously. This is why humanity needs to learn The Lord's Word in increments over time, because while The Lord exists in the past, present and future simultaneously, we are limited to one plane of existence. We as a race (humanity) have existed in the past, exist in the present and will exist in the future but we as single beings exist on one plane of existence. We call it our present. We have a past and a future but in the grand scheme of time the period of our individual existence is so miniscule that it equals the present. Most of us do not have the ability to bend the time / space continuum and go back in time and change things. Most of us do not have the ability to go into the future and see what it holds. Some of us can however, through clairvoyance see into the future and all of us can, to some extent revisit the past through our memories.

The Lord is neither male nor female. The Lord is neither human, nor animal, nor plant, nor mineral. Humanity tends to look at The Lord as a person or being but The Lord is actually a force that can manifest itself as a being but doesn't have to. The Lord is everywhere where life is present. The Lord has a spiritual presence where life is not present. Every living being on this planet and everywhere else has a direct connection to The Lord.

- The Lord has a presence on other planets, in other solar systems and in other galaxies. The Lord is known to many of the beings that live throughout our universe & beyond. The Lord is not known by the same name but The Lord is known and The Lord's presence is felt. The Creation story is not unique to humanity and is common among life forms on many other planets. A resurrection and future return scenario, similar to the Christ story is also common. Not all beings, all of their cultures or all planets know of The Lord or believe in The Lord.

- All living and spiritual beings are endowed with a part of God. We all have a God gene in our DNA, not in our physical DNA, in our spiritual DNA All of the living beings in our universe and beyond are also endowed with The Lord's spiritual DNA.

- One day, scientists will be able to quantify, locate and measure it. Knowing that each living being is endowed with a part of God can help you understand how God works.

The Lord is a puzzle. We are all pieces of the puzzle. We are everyone who is alive, has ever lived and who ever shall live. We are human but we are beyond human. We are plants, animals and every living thing known and unknown to humanity and on planets and galaxies and dimensions beyond our earth.

The part of The Lord that is in our spiritual DNA is in everyone and everything else's spiritual DNA. To save a life is to save a piece of the puzzle. To take a life is to take a piece of the puzzle. Life is precious beyond the value of living. All life is precious in the experience that it brings to the universe and to The Lord.

The Lord is not one being. The Lord is the sum total of all beings, past present and future. The Lord's Time is multifaceted. Past, present and future exist simultaneously. Human time is only lived in the present. That is why The Lord can only be revealed to humankind in increments, because the pieces of the puzzle form a picture in succession and not all of the pieces have been revealed yet, since not all beings have lived yet.

The Lord did not evolve. Humankind's understanding of The Lord did. The Lord has been the same but we as human's only know a little about The Lord. Prophets have given humankind glimpses of The Lord through the ages. Religions have interpreted and rewritten the original writings of The Prophets in an effort to instill the values they believed The Lord (and each particular religion's leadership) wanted to instill in their followers and converts. The Lord's infinite wisdom only allows humanity to get what humanity needs incrementally, depending on the evolution of the human race. These things are revealed through The Lord's Prophets.

A good many humans, judge others not based on God's Law but based on the perception of God's Laws that we have been raised to believe or through study or experience have come to believe. They believe their religion is right and everyone else is wrong. They believe their people shall pass into heaven and all others are doomed to hell. They don't realize and can't even fathom that what religion you are doesn't matter. You don't even have to have a religion to come to The Lord. Everyone comes to The Lord eventually, even atheists. The Lord is beyond the perception of most but not all of us.

The Lord talks to everyone but most people do not know how to listen. Some believe that if they don't hear a voice saying "Okay feeble earthling, this is God talking" The Lord is not talking to them. Others believe that when they go to church or temple that their priest or rabbi or holy man or whatever religious representative they choose, is speaking on behalf of God. They don't truly understand God, they only think they do. There are others, let's call them the enlightened ones, who do listen when The Lord Talks because they have learned how to listen.

The Lord talks to people indirectly through events and through other people and living beings. Often, but not always, The Lord uses a Trilogy to speak to humanity. Messages are often sent in triplicate. They are not often sent by the same messenger. It has been said that The Lord speaks to you first in a whisper, then a shout and then a scream.

To oversimplify how this may work, let's pretend that The Lord is trying to communicate that someone is in danger of having a heart attack. Perhaps the person in question feels a little out of breath when going up some stairs. He may think to himself "Maybe I should see a doctor". He ends up doing nothing. Then, a few days later, a co-worker may say "Are you okay? You look a bit rundown." He hears the words but they don't register as a warning to go to a doctor. Then a few days later he has chest pains. At this point most people would probably get the message.

It has been said and written that The Lord works in mysterious ways. This is true for many. Those who are familiar with the ways of The Lord have a deeper understanding of the beauty and correctness of how The Lord works. It is not as mysterious as it may first seem. The Lord works through living and spiritual beings. These beings act as Agents of The Lord. We have all acted as agents of The Lord at one time or another, often, without realizing it.

Agents of The Lord act on The Lord's behalf. They often do so by transcending their own existence and the infatuations and problems associated with it and reaching out to help others. In the illustration above, the person who told the potential heart attack victim that he looked a little rundown was acting as an Agent of The Lord. People who help others through acts of charity or kindness and especially those who inspire others to help other people and / or other beings are acting as Agents of The Lord.

Oprah Winfrey is a perfect example of an Agent of The Lord because she not only acts on behalf of others she also inspires others to help other people and other beings on a grand scale. She may be a billionaire but she is one person who truly deserves the rewards bestowed upon her. It was a long and sometimes hard journey for her to get where she is today but she overcame adversity and acts selflessly because she has attained enlightenment to some extent.

Since all living things have a part of God in their spirit, harming others is harming a part of God. Killing others is killing a part of God. Helping others is helping a part of God. Kindness for kindness sake can be acting as an Agent of The Lord. Helping those you know and especially strangers, can be acting as an Agent of The Lord. Acts of forgiveness and mercy for others can be acts as Agents of The Lord.

People live and laugh and love. They suffer become sick and die. This is the lot of all living beings. People who choose to live with mere faith and without action live such lives. People who live lives of faith that acts to benefit others live with the power to bestow the blessings of The Lord unto others.

Chapter Two
The Lord Is God of The Universe

"The Lord is God beyond this planet and known to beings all over the universe."

God is Lord of our planet. But God is also Lord of every other planet. God is Lord not only of the people and beings that live on our planet but also the beings that live on every other planet as well. There are many other universes and galaxies. There are millions of planets. There are trillions of living beings. God is Lord of all of them.

God is Lord of the planets, moons and asteroids with life. God is Lord of the planets, moons and asteroids without life. God sends Prophets to many of these planets. The beings living on many of these planets are believers. I, the five Major Prophets who have preceded me, and the seven who shall follow me comprise the 13 sent to the human population on our planet. Other species on our planet also have Prophets. Other planets have different Prophets.

The messages revealed by God to other Prophets on other planets are in most cases, similar to those revealed on our planet. Before I came, the messages were tailored solely to the people of our planet. Since I am the first of two transitional Prophets sent, I am introducing this concept so that humanity can begin to see the bigger picture because that is what humanity needs to move forward towards becoming true citizens of the universe.

My predecessors have said that God is The Lord of the Universe but previous generations of humanity have not been able to fully understand just what that means. Previous generations had never traveled to outer space. They didn't even understand that there is life on other planets and that our planet was not the center of the universe. Those currently alive, through scientific data, have access to the knowledge that there is more in the universe than just us.

I know about this because spiritually, I am part of the stream of consciousness that flows through the universe and although my body has never traveled to other planets, my soul has for my soul has existed since the dawn of time. While I have been following developments on this, my home planet, closely, my soul is also aware of developments on other planets.

People often say if there is life on other planets why haven't they come here and introduced themselves to our leaders? Why haven't they at least tried to communicate with us? First of all how do you know they haven't? Second, humanity has, for several millennia believed that our planet was either the only planet with life on it or that our planet had the most advanced life forms in the universe. Nothing could be further from the truth.

Our species is rather Neanderthal in its development and beings on other planets look at us as a species that needs a lot of development. Why would other beings from more advanced societies want to come all the way over here and work so hard to help us and also have to deal with us?

Chapter Three
The Lord Communicates With Everyone
"Everyone receives messages from The Lord."

The Lord communicates with everyone, but how do you determine what the message is? Some messages are meant for individuals, others for communities. Some messages are obvious, some not so. There are certain things The Lord will never send you a message to do, to kill someone, to rape someone, to molest someone, to bully or harm someone or something. These are all ideas created by the person who is perpetrating them. They may claim "God told them to do it" but they are being deluded into thinking that by something other than God (probably their own ego).

Why, you may ask, are despots allowed to run nations into ruins? There may be no message because the people of that nation allowed that despot to take and hold power. On the other hand, there could be a message to the population of that nation, "You allowed this person to do all this, if you want it to stop, you must stop it."

There are some places in the world that just get hammered by a succession of bad events. Some may ask, "Why does God allow this? " Others may believe that God is punishing the people of that place for past or present evils they have done. In reality, that may not be the message at all. The message may be to the rest of the world "These people need help, why aren't you helping them?"

The Lord's messages are almost often positive and beneficial. They ask you to take a positive action, sometimes benefitting yourself but more often, benefitting others. The Lord takes care of all of us, we just don't always see how. Sometimes The Lord gives a message to another individual who is being asked to act as an Agent of The Lord in a particular instance.

Knowing this can help you learn to read the messages from The Lord that are not always obvious. Instead of waiting for The Lord to come out of the sky and rescue you from your situation, or expecting a voice to come thundering down from the heavens, you can learn to see where your salvation lies by listening to other people who have no reason to point you towards it. You don't need to seek them out; they will seek you out, either from concern or observation.

Often, people who know you and are truly concerned about your welfare will tell you to do something beneficial for yourself. It can be something as simple as "Go on a diet." to as profound as "You need to see your doctor." Most people will ignore those in their lives who advise them to do something that they know is beneficial but that they feel is too difficult or time consuming. What they don't realize is that The Lord often imbues people being used as agents with a sense of urgency or passion, so that they will pass on the message in a way which allows the recipient to really here it. It is often the recipient who ignores the message because they don't perceive it as a potential message from The Lord but as an over concern or even a put down from someone they know cares about them but who's advice and messages they regularly discount. This is one reason you should respect your parents because they often act as Agents Of The Lord on your behalf.

It is important to remember that Agents of The Lord are merely messengers, not psychiatric social workers. They are merely people, not Angels. They deliver the message the best way they know how, often not even knowing they are the Lord's Agent in that instance. They are, therefore, prone to making errors. It is best to listen to the message without judging it by your impression of the messenger.

Chapter Four
The Lord Loves Everybody
"God's love sees beyond imperfections."

    The Lord loves atheists. There is room in The Lord's grand scheme for atheists and non-believers. They do not believe in The Lord but The Lord believes in them. Atheists and non-believers test the faith of believers. In this, they play a necessary role. They walk a different path but their path also leads them to The Lord, they just don't realize it.

    Many have arrived at that particular choice of lifestyle either as a result of something bad happening (loss of faith) and their feeling that The Lord did not intervene on their behalf when they expected The Lord to. Others do not believe because they have the "Doubting Thomas Syndrome". They must see indisputable proof that The Lord exists.

In reality, there is proof all around, they just don't know how to see or verify it. We live in a world of trials and tribulations but also a world of miracles. Miracles, both big and small happen daily. Look for them and, if you look carefully, you will begin to see them.

The Lord loves gay people. Gay people go against most people's norms and most societal norms. They are made to suffer for being different. Sex is merely a biological urge, a very powerful biological urge, granted, but simply a biological urge. Love is what matters. When two people, any two people, love each other, it is a profoundly beautiful thing indeed. The Lord loves all people equally whether they are male, female, or transgender. Many would condemn them to Hell for being gay or bisexual or transgender. The Lord does not. Each person is judged by the God Gene within their spiritual DNA. Sexual orientation is part of each person's determining factors. It is as unimportant as their skin color or race or religion.

The Lord loves everyone you hate. Everyone you have ever hated, because of their character, conduct, race, religion, atheism, sexual orientation, ethnicity, national origin or any other determining factor or trait is loved, honored, cherished and respected by The Lord. In essence, there is only one race that The Lord recognizes from humanity. That is the human race. All of the angry thoughts, condemnations, mistreatments, torturing, murdering and wars started both in the name of mankind but especially in the name of The Lord are quite pointless because we really are all in the same boat.

There are those who will tell you that The Lord does love these people but condemns them to Hell because they don't believe one way or another, or are unenlightened or because they are of lowly character or they are not like "us", the chosen ones. There are others who believe that any of these lowly "others" can be saved if they convert to a particular religion or lifestyle. In reality, no one has to save you, you can save yourself. No one else has the right to judge you because, in the end, through your Perfect Soul, you judge yourself. You save and judge yourself by The Lord's standards, not by the standards of other people, religions or cultures they have created.

The Lord loved all of life so much that all of life is imbued with a part of The Lord. We each have a piece of the Lord's Spiritual DNA within us. Your Spiritual DNA is the nucleus of your original soul. It is the part of you that was around before you had a race or a religion or any prejudice. It is the part of you that knows right from wrong, that knows the truth and knows that we are all one people under the blood. It is the part of you that knows that how you treat any living thing is how you treat The Lord because all living things also have the God Gene in their Spiritual DNA and are also a part of God.

It is the part of you that looks beyond your determining factors and sees what you have been given and what you have done with it. What you have done for yourself, in finding and accomplishing your life's mission, what you have learned from your journey that can enrich that which is The Lord, and what you have done to help other living beings. The rest of the things you have accumulated along the way, the baggage you have chosen to keep, and your ego, all of those are nothing more than gunk stuck onto your Spirit. They are part of what has been clouding up your view of the world but your Perfect Soul, your Spiritual DNA sees your life and its purpose more clearly and is in a better position to judge your accomplishments or lack thereof.

Chapter Five
Religion and Enlightenment
"Religion can lead to enlightenment but enlightenment can be attained without religion."

As I have stated before, I do not come to defile the sanctity of The Word as revealed to The Prophets nor the religions that have been established in their names. I have not come to threaten established religions, and their worldwide communities, past, present or future because I do not come to establish a new religion. In fact, I come to verify their necessity for humanity.

If you want to know what The Lord is, look at the writings of various religions. Not just the Old and New Testament but also the Koran, Bhagavad Gita, the writings of Buddha, Baha'u'llah, the Book of Mormon and a host of others. The Lord is reflected in all of them. They all contribute to (but none of them have a monopoly on) the beautiful tapestry that is God. There are many Prophets who have come before me and many of them have been given part of The Word. The Lord is reflected in their original words as The Lord is reflected here.

Religions provide a framework through which people can anchor their beliefs in The Lord and link them to their daily lives. They provide a social structure through which people can worship The Lord with a community of peers. Many people need a religion and a religious community to help them get through the many opportunities for suffering that life presents.

When the going really gets rough and people have to face dire consequences on their own they do not pray to their church. They do not pray to their priest. They pray to The Lord. They may call The Lord by different names but they are all praying to the same Lord. When people are alone and pray to The Lord that is an example of their direct relationship to The Lord. That is when they turn to the part of The Lord that is in their spiritual DNA and communicate with God directly. Religion may provide the trappings, rituals and ceremonies that people can use as a reference but religion does not provide direct communication. Only being in touch with the part of God in one's spiritual DNA can do that.

It is the development of your direct relationship with The Lord that this volume is concerned with. Everything else is merely trappings and ritual. Trappings and ritual will not take humankind to the next phase of its existence. A world filled with beings that are in touch with the part of The Lord that is in all of them and who act as Agents of The Lord and bestow the blessings of kindness, tolerance, respect and mercy upon each other will.

Developing your relationship with The Lord will make you a better person. The world can change one person at a time. Developed beings won't judge others because they know that only The Lord can judge. They will not hate others because they are of a different race or religion or color, or nation or sexual orientation or socio-economic status because they know that these are merely the trappings of a person as spiritually superficial as the type of clothing that they wear. Developed beings bestowing the blessings of kindness, tolerance, respect and mercy upon others will communicate directly with the part of The Lord that is within those individuals in a way that others on this planet are not able to.

Developed beings within a religious community will, over time change the community to enhance the godly things it is already doing and help change judgmental attitudes held by members of the community. Developed beings who are not in a religious community will serve as a source of inspiration to others who are not in a religious community.

Chapter Six
God is Portable.

"The Lord is always with you and you take The Lord with you where ever you go."

The Lord is Portable. The Lord is always with you. Whether or not you can feel the presence of The Lord, The Lord is always there. When you go places, you take The Lord with you. Through your faith and in the way you personally manifest your faith, The Lord, the idea and concept of The Lord, the effect that The Lord has in your life are transmitted to others. Through those things, The Lord is communicated to and communicates with others.

Through their words and actions, true people of faith, through the power of their faith, communicate the positive power of The Lord unto others. Through their character, their hopefulness when all seems lost, their strength in the face of adversity, their honesty, fairness, social consciousness and their positive attitude even when surrounded by negativity inspire others who are naturally curious about the what gives true people of faith the ability to stay positive, fair, hopeful and strong while others around them are falling apart.

True people of faith introduce more people to the concept of god and inspire more people to believe in God than any media hyped, perceived miracles. This is because miracles, while they may seem rare are actually commonplace. They are usually only known to those who experience them but enough people experience them and actually know people who have experienced them that they are actually underreported by media. They are not miracles to The Lord, only to humankind. True people of faith are not commonplace. They are few and far between. They are scattered everywhere and inspire most of those who know them. They are both within and without religious communities and they inspire people within and without religious communities.

Those who are not true people of faith also take their "version" of god with them wherever they go and communicate that version of God unto others through their words and actions. When they proliferate idle gossip, are mean spirited, jealous, envious, whiners or cruel, they leave an impression on those who know or witness them. They do not leave an impression of what God is. They leave an impression of what their particular belief in God is. In this way, true people of faith a powerful, positive impression of God and of their faith while false people of faith create a negative impression of their faith. Their misdeeds do not stain The Lord but they still do the Lord's work because they create an opening for a more powerful, positive view of The Lord to occupy in the minds of those who know or witness those who are of false faith.

God is portable. The Lord is transported by true people of faith through inspiring example. The Lord is transported by false people of faith as a better alternative.

Chapter Seven
The End is (not) Near

"This is not the end but merely the end of the beginning."

The times in which we currently live are not the end. They are not even the beginning of the end. They are, however, the end of the beginning. Many false prophets have appeared before humankind proclaiming gloom and doom. They cultivate a handful of followers and often coax them to give up their worldly possessions or even their lives. What a waste.

In truth, humanity is closer to the beginning of its tenure on earth than it is to the end. So, all of humankind's excuses for not trying very hard, for polluting the planet, for ignoring or causing disease and catastrophes are pointless. You're stuck with this planet for some time to come. If the air stinks like rotting garbage, the water is viscous and foul, the earth so depleted of nutrients that it yields scrawny, malnourished crops, it's the air you and your future generations will breathe, the water you and they will drink and the soil you and they will sew and the crops you and they will reap.

There is also no need to fear The Lord. Therefore, there is no need to fear hell fire or the boogeyman or anything else coming to make you pay for keeping that library book a couple of days too long. There is no need to do the right thing because you fear that God is going to get you if you don't. Do the right thing because it is the right thing to do. Do the right thing because it may be an opportunity to act as an Agent of The Lord. Do the right thing because it can help propel humanity towards a brighter future and away from the bad air, viscous water and scrawny crop gloom and doom scenario that could come to pass if you don't.

Because The Lord does not judge you directly, but through the piece of Spiritual DNA that is in you, you have an opportunity to exercise the freedom to truly love The Lord and all of creation. You can choose to take advantage of all the wonderful things on this planet, and to live responsibly to ensure that they are around for your lifetime and those of future generations. You can choose to help others instead of just yourself.

In our lifetimes, humanity will begin a shift in thinking, especially in their perception of The Lord. This will begin as a small, possibly insignificant trickle, but over time shall build into a wave on consciousness that sweeps over all of humanity. This shift, when complete, will signal the end of the beginning period and will usher in the beginning of the middle period of humankind's existence.

When the end does come, it will not come as a shout but as a whisper. It will come over a long period of time, as a byproduct of everything that came before it. It will come as a logical successive link in a chain of events that silently evolved before it. Many people read revelations as if it evolves in the span of a two hour action movie. Read it again as if it evolves over a very long period of time. Think of the symbolism as representing things that humankind has done to our planet out of neglect.

Chapter Eight
The Paradigm Shift

"A new day is dawning. There is a revolution within the psyche of humanity."

There is fundamental cultural paradigm shift that is in the process of occurring in the consciousness of humankind. It involves physical and metaphysical belief systems. The supernatural (metaphysical) world view follows that thoughts, intentions and dreams play an important part in how individual lives and indeed, the world at large functions. It is predicated on the power of belief and of faith. Many religions and divine philosophies focus on this belief system. The scientific world view focuses on actions and reactions. It is predicated on hard evidence and proof. It dictates that what is real is what is measureable. For the past several hundred years, there has been a battle ranging between these two belief systems.

The Lord has chosen to reveal these truths now, partly because of this great debate. Humankind has evolved sufficiently to bring them forward. If they were revealed before scientific study had taken enough of a foothold into the psyche of humankind, they would be unintelligible to most people. Now there is enough knowledge and practical experience within the human family to begin to understand, appreciate and apply these truths in our continued evolution.

The concept of "The Lord endowing all living beings with a part of The Lord" merges the two belief systems. The human belief in God has evolved from "There are Many Gods" to "There is Only One God" to "God is God" to "One Special Person is God" and merges into "You Are God" and "Not Only Are You God But Every Other Living Being Is God Too". This equality in sharing a part of God connects all living beings. If there is a part of God in you, you can connect directly with God. You can communicate with God and God can communicate with you. However, your connection is not unique and to constantly remind you of this God communicates with you through agents (events and other living beings) to keep you honest and prevent you from being misled into thinking that you and you alone have this access.

The Wisdom of The Lord is infinite. The Lord always prepares the way. The revelation that all living beings are equipped with a part of God has been touched upon by many religious beliefs but not in the way it is here because humanity was not ready for it yet. Since there is a part of God in all living beings, the way you treat all living beings is the way you treat God. Religious beliefs of kindness and charity in scripture and in practice are the precursors that The Lord has sent to prepare humankind for the information that is being revealed now. The Buddhist respect for all living things, the Christian idea of "what you do to the least of them you do unto me" and the Muslim and Jewish emphasis on tolerance and charity all verify this.

This is why I am confident that what I write here is what is right for humanity now. This is because, it has been revealed now. It doesn't matter to me if only a few people read it and it becomes obscure after that. My faith in The Lord tells me this it is what humanity needs now and it will spread and take root in the psyche of humankind sometime in this millennium, whether or not I am alive to witness it, my soul will witness it and the part of The Lord that is within me will experience it, as will the part of The Lord that is within you.

Chapter Nine
The Beginning

"The Book of Genesis Talks about The Beginning; The Revelations of 2012 Connects it Directly To Our Planet"

In the beginning there was The Lord. And The Lord created Heaven and Earth and all of the planets and stars and galaxies in the Universe. The Lord created atmospheres of various kinds to house different kinds of life forms, which over time would grow and evolve an thrive and perish over time, on various of the planets. The Lord created Souls to breathe life into the various life forms The Lord saw fit to create. And the souls of these beings were kept with The Lord in an ethereal point of space known by many names to many different beings. And these souls would take turns incarnating into different life forms, over periods of time as they wished to or as their karmic debt specified. Each soul to have a particular mission within each particular incarnation but each to also have the global mission of learning through experience and then bringing the experience and what was learned back to The Lord. Which in turn would enrich The Lord and all the other souls in the universe.

Then The Lord created Angels to assist The Lord and Prophets to carry The Lord's word and bring it unto all manner of the beings The Lord created, in increments, over millennia. And The Angels could take to form of whatever being they were sent to assist. And The Lord's Prophets were to be born into an incarnation of whatever manner of creature they were to carry The Word to.

And so it came to pass, that on one planet, in one solar system, in one galaxy was destined to have 13 Major Prophets (along with many minor prophets), to carry The Word unto the planet and to the species which would evolve to become chosen as caretakers of that planet. And The Lord's Prophets would appear, through incarnation in increments that coincided with the evolution of that species to assist that species in understanding The Lord and understanding the responsibilities they had been charged with.

The First of The Lord's Major Prophets came to deliver to humanity, how to attain spiritual liberation through the attainment of knowledge and to liberate oneself from physical and mental attachments. The Second of The Lord's Major Prophets came to give humanity 10 Laws to live by The Third of The Lord's Major Prophets to deliver to humanity what the cause of suffering was and how to eliminate it. The Fourth of The Lord's Major Prophets came to deliver to humanity the elimination of guilt and how to achieve enlightenment through service to others. The Fifth of The Lord's Major Prophets came to deliver to humanity a simple way to worship The Lord. Each of these also delivered unto humanity, either through narration or through the writings of those who followed them, insights on ways to live a better life and to treat and interact with others. Each of these Major Prophets were incarnated to humanity at times of major advancement for humanity. These First Five of The Lord's Major Prophets constitute The Prophets of The Beginning Period, when humanity is considered to be in the childhood of its Intellectual and spiritual evolution.

The Lord shall send to incarnate two Major Prophets with The Word during Humanities Middle Period, The Sixth during humanities transition into early adulthood and has been sent because of humanities scientific advances particularly in genetics and quantum physics. The seventh during humanities culmination of early adulthood. The Eighth, Ninth and Tenth of The Lord's Major Prophets shall be incarnated during humanities middle adult period when humanity shall have spread throughout other planets and be actively engaged with other beings from other planets. The Eleventh and Twelfth of The Lord's Major Prophets shall be incarnated during humanities senior period when humanity shall begin to reach its zenith in intellectual and spiritual achievement. The Thirteenth and final of The Lord's Major Prophets shall be incarnated when humanity has reached its zenith in intellectual and spiritual development. At least one of the Major Prophets shall be female and The Thirteenth Major Prophet could be a repeat incarnation of one of the previous twelve of The Lord's Major Prophets.

Chapter Ten
The Messenger

"The messenger is merely the messenger, not the message."

The Lord utilizes the service of all beings as Agents of The Lord at one time or another to convey messages to or to assist individuals. To carry each installment of The Word, however, The Lord utilizes the services of particular messengers. These messengers are dispatched with the sole purpose of conveying The Word. Most of these messengers don't come to know that they are messengers until many years after their lives have begun. They are allowed to involve themselves in the other endeavors that life has to offer before and after they realize their calling. Often, it becomes more difficult after they put forth The Word. Humankind has a word for these messengers. They are known as Prophets. Prophets are those individuals whom The Lord has entrusted with the keys that open the next door humanity shall step through in its evolution.

There are two types of Prophets: those who foretell future events and those who deliver The Word. The Prophets, who foretell, often foretell events having to do with The Word or a Prophet who will deliver it. Sometimes they also have a message to deliver. Prophets who deliver The Word sometimes have the ability to foretell the future.

There are both Major and Minor Prophets. Major Prophets deliver the part of The Word that is so perfectly times with where humanity is at that it creates a major stream of spiritual consciousness. Minor Prophets deliver a part of The Word that affirms or adds to the stream of consciousness revealed to the Major Prophet or they foretell events that will happen, especially events having to do with a Major Prophet.

Major Prophets are all related. They are not related through physical blood but by Spiritual Blood. Spiritual Blood is the connective virtual tissue between a collective of Perfect Souls that perform a related task. The Major Prophets are a collective. They live separately but exist simultaneously. They draw upon each other for strength during their respective incarnations.

Prophets sometimes enjoy some small level of protection before they deliver The Word. Once The Word has been delivered, however, they are often martyred, usually by people who feel that the new installment of The Word either goes against what they have been taught or might upset an existing power structure. Prophets understand the dangers involved in revealing the installment of The Word that is appropriate for their time (whether humankind realizes it or not), yet they do it anyway. That's how it is with a calling. One is drawn to follow it, despite the risks. This is not because they want to, but because they are compelled to.

A Prophet is mortal, made of flesh and blood and can easily be killed. What the Prophet represents and The Word that The Prophet brings, however, cannot be killed. Those who attempt to destroy the proof of existence of The Prophet cannot destroy The Prophet's legend or legacy. Even those who attempt to destroy The Word that The Prophet brings shall not. Even if they destroy all existing copies of The Word, they won't succeed. They will not find all of them. The copies that they miss will inevitably surface and be spread throughout humanity. Even if someone erases all traces of The Prophet and all copies of The Word, The Lord would just send The Word all at once, through another Prophet or in segments through several Prophets. Despots and armies and empires cannot stop The Will Of God. Trying to, is like a butterfly trying to stop the winds of a hurricane by flapping its wings.

Who I am is unimportant. If you passed me on the street I would pass unnoticed. Just think of me as a messenger. The messenger is never as important as the message. Messengers rarely forget this but others tend to glorify the messenger. Save the Glory for God and for yourself. I don't want it nor do I need it. In essence, who I am is unimportant, the message I convey is.

I am The Lord's Prophet. I am not The Lord. I am both the receiver and the conveyer of The Word. The Word is The Message. The Message is The Great Truth. As a spiritual being I am joined to the message but as a human being I am merely a messenger. As a human being I have hopes, dreams, aspirations and a life that is totally separate from Prophecy. As a human being, I struggle and sometimes fail. As a human being, I am flawed. As a Prophet I am infallible.

I am the sixth major of what will be 13 Major Prophets by the time humanities evolution comes to an end. Like the five who came before me, and the seven who shall follow me, I am here to assist humanity along its path. As a Prophet, I am connected to all others that have come before me and those who shall surely come after me. I do not write this volume because I seek fame or fortune. There are a lot of less dangerous ways to do that. I write this because it is my destiny and because I am compelled to, by forces larger than myself.

I deliver The Word as it has been given unto me. Often, I receive revelations all at once, like a burning, urgent thing I MUST do. They flow through my mind and body and go out my fingers onto my computer keyboard all at once or in segments. They are communicated through what appears to be a stream of consciousness or a vision. The message itself does not change, but the words chosen to convey it may differ slightly from what was received. I do not know why I was chosen, but perhaps it is for my ability to explain complex things in a way that makes them easy to understand.

When the spirit moves me, I simply write what is being revealed to me, either from a vision or at the spur of the moment. The words flow in segments like streams of water after a rain. Over time, these streams begin to join together to create an emergent river of words and ideas and concepts. I do not see the ocean they are flowing into but I know that it's there. I also know that what I write here is forming the nucleus of something great, something that will change everything.

The writing of this, being the recipient and communicator of The Message is not difficult. I have had some of these messages gnawing at me for years but I have resisted the urge to write them down. This may be the human part of me that doesn't want to work at this along with all of the other things I have to do in my life. The power that compels me to write this overtakes me and I put everything else on hold to write. I have pieced these segments together the best I can and have collected them in this volume. I am sure I have made some mistakes; I am, after all, merely a man.

As a Prophet, I do and have always had the gift of Prophecy. I often know what will happen before it happens. I often know things but don't always know them. The gift is sporadic, it comes and goes. I don't know which horse will win a race or what number will come up in the lottery. Although it involves work and in a way is a job, Prophecy is a gift, not an avocation. I still have to hold down a day job to earn my daily bread just like billions of others.

Some may praise me for writing this volume but to them, I say, I am not worthy of your praise. I am merely a guy, doing his job. I am a writer and writing, both this volume and other things I write, is a part of my job, my mission. This volume is part of my mission, my purpose in life. Most of my predecessors haven't written things but inspired others to write things down on their behalf but they all had day jobs too. Their spiritual calling superseded their need to relax from the stresses and strains of daily life. Mine does as well.

The world has not been kind to The Lord's Prophets. We have often suffered cruel fates at the hands of those who fear the potential change that each new installment of The Word brings to the world order and to humanity's perception of The Lord. As those who came before me knew, I know that cruel things could also be awaiting me. This does not matter to me because I have done my job. I have completed the task. The volume is written and is out there for others to read. What happens to me as a consequence may matter to me and my loved ones, but it is really of little importance in the grand scheme of things.

So, to those of you who hate me for what you read here, I can only say this. I am not worthy of your hate. I am not The Lord. I do not claim to be The Lord. I am not The Word. I am not The Message. I am merely The Messenger. I deliver The Message because I am compelled to. The Word is The Great Truth. The Great Truth is The Truth whether or not it is recognized as The Truth. Individual or even collective perception cannot change this reality.

I am both a spiritual being and a human being. I live in two worlds. One is physical, the other spiritual. I live in both worlds simultaneously. I have witnessed and been victim of unspeakable horrors. I have also known joy beyond the perception of many. This is the path I have chosen. The Word offers you an opportunity to live in both worlds as well. The bad things in life happen to everybody. So do the good things. The bad things in life are only as bad as you allow them to be. Changing your perception can change your ability to make sense out of chaos, to learn lessons from events and to weather life's storms. In this way, changing your perception changes your reality.

The Word has come in segments to Prophets throughout the ages. The Word has been specifically formulated for humanity at that moment of our evolution but still has sentiments that resonate with us today and will resonate with us for eternity. Each installment of The Word attracts followers who form organizations called religions.

Religions are nothing more than a life philosophy often centered around The Word as revealed to a particular Prophet.

There is a unity of Prophecy among the five major life philosophies known as Buddhism, Hinduism, Judaism, Christianity and Islam. The Word was revealed to each Prophet differently (Buddha received revelations from his life experiences, Krishna relayed information through conversations with others, Moses received them on a tablet, Jesus had disciples who wrote down his teachings after his death and Muhammad dictated what had been revealed to him to scribes while he was alive) but they each contain universal themes. Some of these themes include being respectful, kind, and righteous. Many other life philosophies and religions have the same themes. For thousands of years humanity has been searching for a way to have universal justice, to end war and poverty and eliminate disease. No matter what life philosophy or religion you follow, be it Eastern or Western, The Lord has given you the answer all along.

As you as an individual, and humanity as a race, progress in your spiritual development you shall come to realize these dreams that people have had since the dawn of time. This installment of The Word and future installments by future Prophets shall help bring both you as an individual and humanity as a race closer to realizing your full potential.

Why is this installment of The Word being revealed now? It is being revealed now because humankind is ready to comprehend it. Changes in humanity's understanding of science (atomic, genetic, environmental, paranormal and quantum physics) as well as worldwide efforts toward social justice and increasing environmental peril indicate that humanity needs another guidepost in its journey.

The world we get now, as in the past and certainly in the future, is a Heaven or Hell of our own making. Don't plan on someone coming down from Heaven to save humanity from the perils of our own toxicity (in thought, deed and environment). The message is clear; we are the caretakers of this planet. We must save the other species divinely entrusted into our care. We must save ourselves. With the understanding humanity currently possesses, we can. Everyone needs to participate.

Be respectful, kind and righteous. Respect other people, their points of view their culture and the environment. Respect other species and our planet while you are at it. Respect The Lord and The Word. Be kind to others. Help people and other species as often as you can. In helping others you can act as an Agent of The Lord. Fight for justice. Not with guns or bombs but with your brains, your talent, your voice and your actions.

Do not praise me for The Word. I am not worthy. Do not hate me for The Word. I am not important enough to hate. Do not hate The Word, even if it differs from some of the things you have been taught. In truth, it complements them. Give The Word a chance and learn the lessons that it is sent to teach you. Know that you live in an age of perceptual shift. The Word has never changed. The only thing that has changed is humankind's ability to perceive it. Humanity is ready to make the shift. Humanity just doesn't know it yet. What is presented to you here will be controversial but will prevail in the end. What is presented to you here will raise more questions than provide answers. But the questions will lead humanity to The Truth, reveal the answers that are waiting in this installment of The Word and will lead to the next.

Chapter Eleven
If You Want To Get Closer To God
"To better understand God, try looking at things from God's perspective."

If you want to get closer to The Lord, consider looking at things from The Lord's Perspective instead of your own. The Lord only recognizes one race of people, the human race. Once you, as an individual do this, you will see how petty all of the cultural and national rivalries and hatreds are. Currently, humanity is like a group of children from the same family squabbling over childish differences.

The time, place and family you are born into are just your beginning criteria, your starting point, so to speak. You are expected to grow beyond them. These beginning criteria, coupled with your determining factors (race, ethnicity, physiological genetics, etc.) have profound influence on the majority of people, some for the entirety of their existence. Many others overcome them in various ways. Through, hard work, luck and concentrated efforts people are able to rise above poverty, conquer disabilities, and reach beyond the barriers imposed by prejudice. People can also go beyond that by transcending the limitations of their culture and nation in their world view and in their religion in terms of their spiritual growth.

Religion is a good thing. Religions were founded in an effort to understand The Lord and live in a way that is pleasing to The Lord. Religions are the structure upon which most people frame their knowledge of The Lord and partake in worship through a religious community. No one religion, however, explains everything. No one religion has all the answers. No one religion has all of the pieces to the puzzle.

This is because religions are evolutionary. They were not founded by Prophets but by their followers. Prophets do not come to found religions but to deliver the next pieces of the puzzle that humankind assembles to understand The Lord. Religions have pieces to the puzzle, but since all of the pieces of the puzzle have yet to be revealed to humankind, no one religion or even all of the world's religions have the completed puzzle.

Since religions are evolutionary, one can, through study, research various religions and find one that has the puzzle pieces and world view that fits one's own beliefs. Many people simply follow the religion they were born into and look no further. True spiritual awakening, however, takes place through investigation and comparison. That is why the priests (or their counterparts) in many religions study various religions so that they can be sure the religion they are representing agrees with them and so that they can have insightful discussions with followers of their religion or potential converts from other religions.

Know also, that following the teachings of Jesus, Moses, Mohammad, Buddha or any of the other thousands of Prophets who have come forth and shall continue to come forth to light the path of humanity is enlightening but is only partially. The Lord is beyond your perception and beyond the perception of any one religion. Therefore, following one particular religion will provide structure but will also impose limitations. There are always unexplained areas, always mysteries or cop outs ("This is an illusion and not something you should waste your time and energies on").
Following the teachings of only one Prophet is ensuring that you will miss much of the beauty and wisdom that is The Lord while missing much of the point of your existence.

Psalms
Prayers and spiritual songs.

Your Word

I was hungry and your word fed me
I was tired and your word energized me
I was weak and you word gave me strength
I was lonely and your word befriended me
I was sick and your word healed me
I was depressed and your word uplifted me
I was afraid and your word gave me courage
I was without a home and your word sheltered me from the storm
I was lost and your word showed me the way to go
I was angry and your word made me peaceful
I was powerless and your word empowered me
I was stagnant and your word transformed me
I was ignorant and your word enlightened m
What You Have Done for Me, Lord
I was an orphan in the house of humanity
And you adopted me
I was afflicted with the maladies of a beaten down life
And you transformed me
I saw the world as a child, transfixed upon my own ego

And you showed me the world beyond myself
I was idle
And you showed me the work to be done
I was boastful
And you showed me the power of humility
I was hopeless
And you showed me the miracles that are all around me
I wallowed in the filth of my own desire
And you cleansed me
I was ashamed
And you told me that I had nothing to be ashamed of
I was guilty
And you showed me limitless forgiveness
I was alone
And you befriended me
I felt unworthy
And you rebuilt my self respect
I was numb
And you breathed new life into my soul
I was powerless
And you empowered me

God Is Love

VERSE 1
God is love
God is peace
God is beauty
In man and plant and beast
God is justice
God is compassion
God is beyond all things that you can imagine
Cause God is love
CHORUS
God watches over me
Guides me towards the path of right
Wraps loving arms around me
And cherishes my life

VERSE 2
God is hope
God is faith
We are the benefactors
Of all that God creates
God is our future
God is our past

The One and only
The first and the last
And God is love
(Repeat Chorus)
BRIDGE
God is caring
God is sharing
God is strength
God is faith
God is the smile
On the face of humankind
God is the uplifting thought
That just went through your mind
VERSE 3
God is hope
God is wisdom
God's in your friends
Whenever you need them
God is salvation
God is our friend
God is all that's good
God's love never ends
Cause God is love
(Repeat Chorus)
END BRIDGE
God is the life force

God is above
God is all around us
Cause God is love

Hope Is The Answer

VERSE 1
Man is an employee
Working and sweating every single day
Doesn't have much money
Still he's got bills to pay
He questions the master
And has a long wait for his reply
Just when He's going to give up
Comes the revelation
That hope is the answer
When all else fades away
VERSE 2
Woman is a mother
She's got a lot of mouths to feed
Feels like a martyr
Frustration is what she bleeds
So many disappointments
Yet her faith it keeps her strong
Kids need someone to look up to
In times of desperation
Hope is the answer
VERSE 3

So much suffering and heartache
Bourne upon this worldly plain
So many caught up in it
That can't see beyond their pain
Cries the Wisdom of the ages
All wounds are healed in time
Like a beacon to the future
Shines the inspiration
That Hope is the answer

To Be Loved

VERSE 1
What a warm feeling it is
To be held
To be touched
To be cared for with tender affection
But most of all to be loved
Once I saw a rich man
Sink to his knees and begin weeping
He built a mighty empire of concrete and steel
But without love, he was nothing
We all want to be loved
VERSE 2
When the night is cold and you are weary
And the burdens that you carry too much
It's a special kind of comfort
To know that you are loved
Soon the problems that you have seem petty
And the shackles around your soul melt away
And the love that you feel surrounds you
And somehow gives you strength
We all want to be loved
Bridge

The rich man can lose his fortune
The man of power can become corrupt
But it's the wise man who knows the secret
To happiness is to be loved
We all want to be loved

Time For Love

VERSE 1
A time for letting the sunshine into our lives
A time for laughter in the rain
A time to realize that beauty comes in all colors
A time for ending all the pain
CHORUS
There's something deep
In the heart and soul of the people
Crying out, "We've had enough".
Time for all, to join together as one
Lord, now's the time
Time for love
VERSE 2
A time to lay back and enjoy one another
A time to stand up for what we believe
A time for real leaders to step out of the shadows
A time for real emotions to be set free
CHORUS
There's something deep
In the heart and soul of the people
Crying out, "We've had enough".
Time for all, to join together as one

Lord, now's the time
Time for love

Your Love Is Like Sunshine

VERSE 1
Some loves are like a candle
Romantic but lacking strength
Some loves are like a streetlamp
By the light of dawn their glory fades
Some loves are like a light house
A beacon through stormy times
But your love surpasses all of these
Cause your love defeats the night
CHORUS
 Your love is like sunshine
Lighting my life with your word
Your love is like sunshine
It's a comfort just knowing
You are with me Lord
 (Repeat)
VERSE 2
Some loves are born of physical lust
When the passion fades the love grows cold
Some loves are born of convenience
Inconvenience makes them explode
Some loves are born of the spirit

Others are born of the mind
But your love is supernatural
Your love's beyond space and time
(Repeat Chorus)

My God

My God doesn't demand people follow orders like robots and doesn't threaten people with eternal damnation to keep them in line because those are egotistical actions and My God isn't egotistical.

My God doesn't punish people for disobeying My God provides learning opportunities so that they may learn lessons and improve their behavior through a higher understanding instead of out of fear of punishment.

My God doesn't stand silent when people's lives seem to be falling apart, My God communicates with people through The Word, through events and through other people who deliver messages.

My God hasn't given one group of people an exclusive on The Word. My God hasn't reserved an eternal home for the chosen few. My God welcomes everyone who wants to get to know God better.

My God is an equal opportunity lover and loves all living beings equally no matter what form they take. All life is precious to My God and a kindness to any life form is a kindness to God. Taking the life of any life form is taking a part of God that the taker does not have the ability to restore.

My God doesn't judge people by their race, or religion or sexual orientation or economic status because My God knows that these are things all people are born with, a starting point. My God doesn't look at where you start. My God looks at how you have grown beyond your starting point and what you have learned from the experience we call life.

My God doesn't need pass judgment upon humankind because My God has given a spiritual gene to all people and an objective part of that gene allows all spirits to pass judgment upon themselves.

My God understands that humanity can only understand things when given information they can comprehend. This information is called The Word. My God sends prophets to deliver The Word at times which parallel humanities advancements and ability to understand more. Although God remains the same, The Word is ever changing as new information is added to what humanity knows as humanity has advanced enough to understand it.

My God understands that humanity can only understand things given the information they can comprehend. This information is called The Word.

My God sends prophets to deliver The Word at times which parallel humanities advancements and ability to understand more. Although God remains the same, The Word is ever changing as new information is added to what humanity knows as humanity has advanced enough to understand it.

My God's will is always done and My God always wins because My God exists in the past, present and future simultaneously. My God is the master of time and can change any outcome, at any time during the past, present or future.

My God has a master plan in which every soul has a role. My God has a mission for each and every person. My God has provided tools for each individual; to find out what their mission is.

My God is your God. My God is the same God you have been praying to no matter what your religion. If you think you know everything about God and you didn't know some or all of these things, do you really know God?

To find out more google The Prophet of Life Ministries.

Author Biography
The Prophet of Life

I am a journalist, author and songwriter. I write the Faith and Spiritual books as well as topical, thematic literature books for Love Force International Publishing.

I have had very broad and varied life experiences and those experiences enrich my writing. I write on Spiritual topics as well as topics of global importance. I write non-fiction that tells it like it is but that is solution oriented as opposed to just complaining about things. I have books on topics such as Crime and Punishment, Racism, and Faith.

I like writing things from unique perspectives. I like to challenge my reader's perceptions and allow them to come away with new insights. If a lesson can be woven into the fabric of the written word, so much the better but the lesson is often subtle.

I try and see things the way they are and the way that they can be. This allows me to see the possibilities within various situations both in my life and in the things I write. As a result, I can often add twists and turns readers will not likely see coming in fiction I write. I can often communicate things from unique and different perspectives and see solutions to problems and issues that I communicate about in my nonfiction.

I am not afraid to take risks both in my life and in

my writing. I have tackled controversial issues in both. My nonfiction Word Press blog, Insight, a blog by The Prophet of Life, is full of examples. I have an offbeat sense of humor and have written humorous things as well as serious. I started a You Tube Channel and now have over 100 videos that have words and music but no pictures. Despite the fact that there are no pictures over 150,000 people from 210 different nations have viewed the videos on my You Tube channel.

I enjoy hearing from my readers. I enjoy writing. I hope you will find my books interesting and entertaining.

Kindle Books by Love Force International Publishing

Whether you are interested in true stories, fiction, humor, action, adventure, spiritual insights, quotes, poetry, self-help or children's books, Loveforce International Publishing has got you covered. **Our 99 cent commitment,** our commitment to a 99 cent (U.S.) price for all our kindle e book titles keep our books affordable. Since our books sell for the local equivalent of 99 cents (U.S.) in other global markets, people around the globe can afford them. Our books do sell all over the world. Our 99 cent commitment means there has never been a better time to stock up on books published by Love Force International! At a time when many paperbacks sell for $13.95-$17.95, our paperbacks sell for between $6.50-$7.50 (U.S.). This too is a bargain for our readers.

Many of the books listed here include their Amazon Kindle ASIN code. Typing an ASIN code into any Amazon search bar should bring that title up. If you are looking for titles published by Loveforce International Publishing you can simply type Loveforce International Publishing Company into any amazon search bar anywhere in the world and many of our books will come up. For books in Spanish type Loveforce Libros en Espanol into any Amazon search bar anywhere in the world.

Many of our books have Spanish Language versions. We didn't just slap the text onto Google Translate and pray. We worked with a professional Spanish translator born and raised in a Spanish speaking nation. We made our authors available to that person to clarify idioms and other translation glitches so that our Spanish versions are not only close to the original in meaning but they also fit within the culture(s) of Spanish Speaking nations.

We have some promotional videos for our books on Amazon Kindle. You can find many others on our You Tube channel The Loveforce International Publishing channel. Just type Loveforce International Publishing into your You Tube search bar anywhere in the world and the channel will come up along with many of our videos. Our logo is a photo of the sun coming out through a cloud over a mountain top. We have a Spanish Language You Tube Channel as well. Type Loveforce International Publishing en Espanol and you will see some of our Spanish language videos from our Loveforce enEspanol channel come up with the ones in English.

NOTE: Books with ASINs are available now the others will be available soon. All Titles are printed in English. Books with an **SP** after the title also have a version translated into Spanish. A List of Paperbacks will be below, Reader Series books with a paperback version will have **Ppr** on the same line as the title.

The Reader Series is a series of readers that are a sampling of writings by one or more authors.

The Prophet of Life Reader (7 Book Sampler) Volumes 1 & 2

What do essays, articles, stories, poetry and quotes have in common? They are all in this sampling of stories, poems and other writings from 7 of The Prophet of Life's writings found in these Kindle books.

Author: The Prophet of Life   **ISBN:** 978-1-936462-07-0   **ASIN:** B015D716C0 (Vol 1)   **ASIN:** B06XBSWKX8 (Vol 2)

The Mark Wilkins Reader 7 Book Sampler! Volumes 1 & 2

One story from seven books by Mark Wilkins. Whether its smart spouses, inquisitive fools, teachers, gangsters or ghosts these books give you a good sampling of stories by the man known throughout the world as A Storyteller. Within its pages you will find horror, humor and pathos.

 Author: Mark Wilkins   **ISBN:** 978-1-936462-38-4   **ASIN:** B01MU0Z51H **Volume 1**

The Love Force International Reader 7 Book Sampler! 4 Books in This Series

Whether you want fiction, humor, children's stories, poetry or quotes these books have got all of those and more! A sampling of 7 different books by three authors offered in Kindle books published by Love Force International.

Edited by Evan Lovefire   Vol 1 **ASIN: B06XBHD9RX**
Vol 2 **ASIN: B06XBMGLNK**
Vol 3 **ASIN: B07DCGTLKF**   Vol 4
ASIN: B07DP51BWG

The Love Force International Sampler, Spanish Books Edition SP Volumes 1 & 2
These books contain a sampling of 7 different books by three authors translated into Spanish. The books translated include What Faith has Taught me, Controversy, True Stories of Inspiration & General interest and Quotes about God by The Prophet of Life, Stories of The Supernatural, Slices of Life How to Become The Person You've Always Wanted by Mark Wilkins and Classic Children's Stories You've Likely Never Heard, and my first & second books of stupid little fables by Dr. Goose.
Edited by C. Gomez Vol 1 **ASIN:** B06XB3RJ2K Vol 2 **ASIN:: B07F2PLVHF**

The True Stories Series is a series of books which include true stories.

True Stories!   **SP**

A riveting collection of true stories. Whether you want to know about the toddler taken by a gator at a Disney Resort, an 18 year old who doesn't exist, which popular restaurant chain has a corporate mentality of public humiliation for its employees or an alarming new trend that could affect your household this book has got it all and they are all absolutely true!

Author: The Prophet of Life   **ISBN: 978-1-936462-16-2**
ASIN: B06XVSZSZ9

True Stories: Inspiration and General Interest
                    SP

What do cell phone addicts, George Orwell, birds, Paul McCartney, The Nobel Prize, Black Friday, Led Zeppelin, garbage, a pep talk, tipping, Steve Jobs, Shakespeare, inspirational thoughts and your mother have in common? They are in true stories in this book. True Stories of Inspiration & General Interest brings together stories and poems about celebrities, trends and everyday people. Sometimes surprising, always interesting, it will entertain you and give you something to think about at the same time.

Author: The Prophet of Life   **ISBN: 978-1-936462-15-5**
ASIN: B00TXWVNUC   ASIN: B01BBCKFZU (Spanish Edition)

Controversy

                              Ppr SP

What do Caitlyn Jenner, Donald Trump, a cure for AIDS, Chinese hackers, Adolf Hitler and Global Warming have in common? They are all at the heart of a controversy and there are stories about them in this unique book that turns tabloid headlines inside out. **Author:** The Prophet of Life
**ISBN: 978-1-936462-19-3 ASIN: B016MWU8NS
ASIN: B01CRF3098 (Spanish Edition)**

True Stories of Crime and Punishment
SP
This book of serious crime stories is ripped from headlines all over the globe. From the family that vanished, to the 11 year old girl killed in a fight over a boy, to the prisoner who hasn't eaten in 14 years, to the severed human head found near the famous Hollywood sign these stories ripped will astound you and give you pause to think.
Author: The Prophet of Life **ISBN: 978-1-936462-17-9
ASIN: B01406YZBE ASIN: B01N10ND7S (Spanish Edition)**

Strange but True!
A collection of facts and stories about people, places and things that are strange and seem like fiction but are absolutely true!
Author: Mark Wilkins **ASIN:**

The A Storyteller Series is a unique book series. Instead of concentrating on a particular character or genre, the series consists of collections of short stories by Author Mark Wilkins, Also Known As A Storyteller.

The Slice of Life Series are books with humorous stories.

Slices of Life Volume 1
                    SP
is a collection of humorous short stories about life. Most of them deal with marriage and family members. From smart spouses to intelligent little children to guys trying to impress their friends and in-laws trying to master technology each story is like a little slice of life but together, they make up an irresistible pie. Sit back, grab a cup of coffee and enjoy some slices of lie because, before you know it, you will have finished the whole thing.
Author: Mark Wilkins **ISBN: 978-1-936462-11-7 ASIN: B014ZF5VY0   ASIN: B01BBBZUL0 (Spanish Edition)**

Slices of Life Volume 2
                    SP
This sequel to Slices of Life has more humorous stories about the rich, the poor and the middle class. It even has a story about one of their pets. Ignorance is the main theme of this book, ignorance that has consequences that are sometimes touching but always humorous. So brew so coffee or tea, sit down and relax and enjoy another satisfying batch of more slice of life because, before you know it, you will have devoured the whole thing.
Author: Mark Wilkins **ISBN: 978-1-936462-12-4 ASIN: B01M2B3YZ1   ASIN: B06XKP5C66   (Spanish Edition)**

The Stories of The Supernatural Series are books with scary stories that cross the spectrum of Horror, Occult, Ghost, Monster and Fantasy genres.

Stories of The Supernatural Volume 1 SP

Ghosts, demonic creatures, and Death. This collection of Short Stories will haunt and entertain you. Whether it's the classic evil of A Lump of Coal or the whimsy of A Ghost in the House this collection of Short Stories and poems will haunt, thrill and entertain you. **Author:** Mark Wilkins **ISBN:** 978-1-936462-18-6 **ASIN: B01M1N1QR5   ASIN: B01MA12YXY (Spanish Edition)**

Stories of The Supernatural Volume 2 SP

In this sequel to Stories of The Supernatural there are more Ghosts, Demonic Creatures and Death. This collection of short stories Centers of Ghosts and Monsters. Within its pages you will marvel at the exploits of The Soul Collector, Shudder at the mention of the dreaded Bungadun and of the Hell Banger and ride the rails on the ghost train. Strap on your seat belts, it's going to be a bumpy ride! **Author:** Mark Wilkins **ISBN:** 978-1-936462-26-1 **ASIN: B01MDJMSUY ASIN: B01M4FXDL1   (Spanish Edition)**

A Storyteller Series Continued...
The A Week's Worth of Fiction Series is a series of books with seven stories of fiction each. Each book has stories organized by a particular theme. In a unique twist, each story is followed by a poem which has something indirectly to do with the story that came before it. Readers are asked to read one story and poem that follows it per day. This gives them one day to see how the story resonates with them and try and figure out how the poem is related to the story. To end the suspense, the author includes a section called "How the Poems in this Book are related to the Stories" at the end of the book.

A Week's Worth of Fiction Volume 1
SP

In Volume 1 of A Week's Worth of Fiction, People on The Edge, you will meet people on the edges of society. A security guard who struggles with a dying wife, an elderly man whose cast aside and left to die, one woman struggling to capture romance before her beauty fades and another struggling with cancer. You will meet a little boy who terrorizes a grocery store, a teenage boy searching for love and a small businessman struggling against a monopoly. If you want fictional stories you will never forget you only need to count to 7. **Author:** Mark Wilkins   ISBN: 978-1-936462-13-1
ASIN: B01521SQ02   ASIN: B06XVD21PM (Spanish Edition)

A Week's Worth of Fiction Volume 2
SP

Volume 2 of A Week's Worth of Fiction, Science Fiction you will be intrigued and astounded by stories about a girl who has the cure for a deadly disease, a woman on a date with psycho somatic disease called prophecy, a robot chicken, a supernatural fly, an astral projection, a teacher in a new job where everything is not what it seems and a futuristic world where the only economy is barter. If you want science fiction stories you will never forget you only need to count to 7. **Author:** Mark Wilkins
ISBN: 978-1-936462-14-8 ASIN: B01LX9RZH7
ASIN: B071GCYFK6 (Spanish Edition)

A Week's Worth of Fiction Volume 3
SP

A Week's Worth of Fiction Volume 3, The Many Sides of Violence, features 7 fictional stories that explore violence. One story looks at what goes through the mind of a terrorist about to blow himself up. Another, looks at an executive considering suicide. The plots of other stories include a, man trying to outwit an armed carjacker, a sky marshal trying to figure out which passage is a terrorist, a soldier who realizes someone in his platoon is a serial killer, an ex-convict who has to decide if he should use violence to combat evil and an everyman who becomes a hero through unspeakable violence, if you want violent stories you will never forget you only need to count to 7.**Author:** Mark Wilkins
ASIN: B071WNC6ZX   ASIN: B072K6J9HN (Spanish Edition)

A Week's Worth of Fiction Volume 4
SP

In A Week's Worth of Fiction 4, Realizations, you will meet people from various backgrounds who come to important realizations. You will meet a Doctor who comes to a realization about old age, a politician who struggles to be his own man, a rich man who reaches an epiphany after a chance encounter at a store, A farmer in need of help, A little boy who struggles with a new cell phone that seems processed, a swimmer who gains insight from her morning routine and a police officer who develops empathy for a hardcore gangster. If you want the fictional stories you will never forget you only need to count to 7. **Author:** Mark Wilkins **ASIN: B07217QL6H**   **ASIN: B071JVQQ96   (Spanish Edition)**

A Storyteller series continued...
The Classroom Confessions Series is a series of books with stories from the front line of public education. Stories and song lyrics mostly focus on students and teachers. Some will make you laugh, others will make you cry but they will all give you insights into public education and entertain you while giving you something to think about.
Classroom Confessions Volume 1
  SP
is a series of true stories from the front lines of public education. Within its pages you will meet quirky characters, the good, the bad and the over caffeinated. Some of them are teachers, some students and some are administrators. Some will make you laugh, others will make you cry but they all play an important role in public education. Their stories are written in way that will entertain you and give you something to think about.
Author: Mark Wilkins **ISBN: 978-1-936462-08-7 ASIN: B00VNFJBX8   ASIN: B01MSV4N92 (Spanish Edition)**

Classroom Confessions Volume 2
  SP
 Is another series of true stories from the front lines of public education. Within its pages you will meet unforgettable characters like the French Substitute, Mr. Happyhands, Harry Winkwater, The Bushwhacker and of course, Julian. Some will touch your heart, others will give you something to think about but they will all entertain you. **Author:** Mark Wilkins **ASIN: B01N1OCRVC ASIN: B06XC9HDQV (Spanish Edition)**

The Love Force Novella Series: These are short novels of varying length.

Karma   **Ppr SP**

The story of one man who negotiates between two different cultures, and opposing life views competing for his attention. His conflicts and struggles are overshadowed by cosmic forces he cannot understand. Karma provides insights into the struggles and conflicts we all face.

Author: Mark Wilkins
ASIN: B0722R448R (English Edition)
ASIN: B072Z6L36 (Spanish Edition)

The Beyond Faith Series
Is a series of books that look at life from a spiritual perspective. No matter what your faith, you will find spiritual insights in these books that will enrich your life.
What Faith Has Taught Me
SP

I am just an ordinary person who has been privileged to have a life filled with miracles and revelations. There are many times when I had nothing except faith but faith was all I needed to sustain me. My faith and my God have taught me many life lessons. This book shares some of the things my faith has taught me and the spiritual insights I have gained because of my faith. **Author:** The Prophet of Life   **ISBN: 978-1-936462-03-2   ASIN: B01527IKT8 ASIN: B01EE3QSW2   (Spanish Edition)**

Finding God in A Chaotic World   SP
The world can seem so chaotic these days. Many people long for guidance. Many others want to get closer to God. How do you find God amidst the chaos and confusion? How can you discern God's messages from the multi-media blitz we are each bombarded with every day? Some people are part of an organized religion. Others are spiritual without a particular religion. Some are still searching, All of them trying to find God.

In this book, you will learn that The Lord communicates with how The Lord communicates with you. You will learn about the True Nature of God and realize just how profound God's Love and reach are. You will learn the secret of why God's will always prevails. If you are ready for revelations that may change the way you look at life in general and your life in particular, read this book.
Author: The Prophet of Life **ISBN: 978-1-936462-01-8**
ASIN: B00SLLZAAU
ASIN: B0793KDYX3 (Spanish Edition)

Finding God without Religion   **SP**
People of faith are not exclusive to religion. There are many who are spiritual or agnostic. They don't fit into the doctrine, rituals and congregational community of religion. In this wisdom filled volume, people of faith but without an organized religion can gain insights into life, the afterlife and God without being brow beaten or guilt tripped into conversion. This volume is Book 2 of the Revelations of 2012 Beyond Faith series. Part 1 is entitled Finding God in A Chaotic World.
Author: The Prophet of Life **ISBN: 978-1-936462-10-0**
ASIN: B00XKPD86K   **ASIN: B07F5MTFVQ**
(Spanish Edition)

Inspiration For All 1
            SP

Selected Inspirational Writings. Whether you are of faith or just in need of inspiration in your life, this book full of inspirational stories, poems and essays will sustain and strengthen you on your journey. **Authors: The Prophet of Life & Mark Wilkins ASIN: B071ZM17V6**
ASIN: B071JW8XXH (Spanish Edition)

Inspiration for All 2
      SP
This is a book of selected inspirational writings by three different authors. It will not only entertain you but will also stimulate your mind by offering you alternative ways of looking at things and opportunities to gain insights. **Authors**: Mark Wilkins, The Prophet of Life & Dr. Goose. **ASIN: B0736JH6M9**   **ASIN: B072WK9JBH (Spanish Edition)**

Outrageous Humor Series
Books of stories and fake news articles for those with an off-beat sense of humor.

Outrageous Stories   SP
This book is filled with offbeat humor articles. All of them are fictitious and many of them completely outrageous. No one is safe from being made fun of be they terrorists, Presidents, Dictators, The Movie and Record Business or couch potatoes. If you are college age or older and have an offbeat, irreverent, sense of humor, this book is for you!
Author: Mark Wilkins **ISBN: 978-1-936462-33-9**
ASIN: B01LY3VZJR
ASIN: B07D1RH9W3 (Spanish Edition)

More Outrageous Stories   SP
This book is filled with more offbeat humor articles. All of them are fictitious and many of them completely outrageous. No one is safe from being made fun of be they terrorists, Racists, National Holidays or the medical establishment. If you are college age or older and have an offbeat, irreverent, sense of humor, this book is for you!
Author: Mark Wilkins **ISBN: 978-1-936462-33-9 ASIN: B074Y8LTTJ**

Self Help Series
This consists of books by different authors designed to help people improve their lives.

Become The Person You've Always Wanted to Be
SP

This self-help book offers a simple, yet profound method of making positive changes in your life. It includes a link to download exclusive, helpful companion worksheets to help you become the person you have always wanted to be.
Author: Mark Wilkins **ISBN:** 978-1-936462-39-1
ASIN: B01MSYVAB6   **ASIN: B01MSYVU6R**   **(Spanish Edition)**

Life Success Kit   **SP**
Spiritual Thought Leader The Prophet of Life helps you clarify what success really means to you through a series of inspirational life lessons designed to give you new perspectives on achieving success and a blueprint for making changes in the things that are preventing you from becoming a success.
Author: The Prophet of Life   **ASIN: B01MZ2TSCP**
    ASIN: B078JZGWDH (Spanish Edition)

The Your Life in Rhyme Poetry Series
Is a series of Poetry books unlike any you have ever read whether it is an exploration of life itself through a thematic chapter on each of the various stages of life as in Reflections in The Mirror of Life, The mixture of thought provoking essays and inspirational poetry of Black in America or the exploration of a single topic as in Romance Returns or Life in Verse. The books in this series will have you rediscovering poetry in a way that will make you wonder why you ever avoided it in the first place.

Reflections in the Mirror of Life
This unique book explores life through its harsh realities, pleasant diversions and positive possibilities. The book looks at modern society, the problems it faces, and the people who are a part of it. In a unique twist that's different from most books of poetry, Reflections is divided into five chapters, each of which explores a different theme woven into the fabric of modern life. The tone for each chapter is set by a free verse poem which is followed by a series of rhyming poems on that theme.
Author: The Prophet of Life **ISBN:** 978-1-936462-04-9
ASIN: B00V2TSAXC

Black in America

is an exploration of racism through essays and poems. It spans from the beginnings of the Civil Rights movement through today. It looks at people who have been lightning rods for race relations in America and has some surprising insights into the people and events that have shaped race relations in America for the past 60 years. This book is a good companion for anyone who wants to gain insight into the Civil Rights movement, race relations and racism itself.   **Author:** The Prophet of Life
ISBN: 978-1-936462-09-4   ASIN: B00S05QSXA

- **Every Lyric Tells A Story   SP**
A collection of unique song lyrics that tell compelling stories about people, their lives, their hopes and dreams. You can find yourself and people you know in many of them. **Authors:**   The Prophet of Life & Mark Wilkins   ASIN: B01NAFDWZW
ASIN: B07F5N1Y5G (Spanish Edition)

Romance Lives!
Romance Lives is a very special collection of Romantic Love Poems. The poems are arranged to follow the arc of a romance from its early, puppy love stages through its sweet seductions and the blissful wisdom of mature love. If you are searching for Romance in your love relationship or just want some joyful, insightful romantic reading this book is for you! **Authors: The Prophet of Life & Mark Wilkins   ASIN: B07D9WY6V5**
ASIN: B07DP7HX9P (Spanish Edition)

Life in Verse

A collection of poems about life. The poems and song lyrics are about people, their lives, their hopes and dreams. You can find yourself and people you know in many of them. **Author:** The Prophet of Life   **ASIN:**

The Best Quotes quotation series

Is a series of books filled with quotes attributed to the Prophet of Life whose quotes have been used by charities, corporations, institutions of Medicine and higher learning. The book includes a license to use any of the quotes as long as they are attributed to The Prophet of Life.

The Best Quotes About God   SP

This short book is filled with some of the more popular quotes about God attributed to The Prophet of Life. It is both thought provoking and inspirational. It is filled with dozens of quotes about God that one can read and copy for personal use. **Author:** The Prophet of Life **ISBN: 978-1-936462-20-9 ASIN: B018P0M8OC   ASIN: B01BJXYHLY (Spanish Edition)**

The Best Quotes on General Subjects
SP

This short book is filled with some of the more popular quotes on general subjects attributed to The Prophet of Life. The book includes quotes on topics such as life, love, happiness, crime and punishment, wellness and includes many of the humorous quotes attributed to The Prophet of Life. You will find the wit and wisdom in its pages thought provoking and inspirational. It is filled with dozens of quotes about God that one can read and copy for personal use.

Author: The Prophet of Life   **ASIN: B01M58L9LW**
ASIN: B01M58L9LW (Spanish Edition)

The Best Spiritual Quotes
   SP
This book is filled with some of the more popular quotes on Spiritual Subjects attributed to The Prophet of Life. Included are quotes on faith, mercy, life lessons, humanity and spirituality. You should find them to be profound, thought provoking and inspirational. It is filled with many pages of quotes that one can read and copy for personal use. **Author:** The Prophet of Life
ASIN: B01MQVA87Q

Children's Storybook Series
We offer a good selection of Juvenile & Children's books in both prose and rhyming verse.

Classic Children's Stories You've Likely Never Heard SP
Help develop your child's creative abilities and develop their imagination by reading them stories from this book that has no illustrations. Whether it's a story about Prince trying to find the answer to a question, a spider talking about a savior, a kingdom in trouble or a child trying to save the world you will find yourself wanting to read these children's stories with international flavor again and again. This first book in the series is for smaller children.
Author: Dr. Goose
ISBN: 978-1-936462-40-7   **ASIN:** B01NAF8QNU
       ASIN: B01MR5PR84   (Spanish Edition)

More Classic Children's Stories You've Likely Never Heard   SP
This sequel gives you more unknown classics. The book introduces new characters like a little chicken whose life is similar to a person's and a ballad about a hairy man. There is a story about a prince whose refusal causes an international incident. There is even an updated version of classic children's story everyone knows from different character's points of view. This second book in the series helps tweens and juvenile children creative abilities and develop their imagination as stories from this book that has no illustrations either. **Author:** Dr. Goose **ISBN: 978-1-936462-41-4**

ASIN: B074Y8G4JZ ASIN: B0755YK6NH (Spanish Edition)

My First Book of Stupid Little Fables SP
Whether the greed of mooches and lunch thieves, sadistic children, or bizarre stories about pets this first installment in the series of irreverently humorous stories with twisted endings about the selfish and the greedy delivers. It even has the stupid little drawings! For Juveniles. **Author:** Dr. Goose
ISBN: 978-1-936462-44-5 ASIN: ASIN: (Spanish Edition)

My Second Book of Stupid Little Fables SP
Whether it's well-meaning but incompetent grandmas, egotistical women, sadistic children, or crazy people in shopping centers, this second installment in the series of irreverently humorous stories with twisted endings about the selfish and the greedy delivers. It even has the drawings you love to make fun of just like the first one! For Juveniles. **Author:** Dr. Goose   **ISBN:** ASIN: ASIN: (Spanish Edition)

More Children's Stories
School Kidz Volume 1 Elementary and Middle School SP
Six funny stories about kids who are smarter than their age. Within its pages you will meet A boy whose vocabulary is better than the adults in his school, a kid who escapes a spanking, A kid who gets a new cell phone with a built in problem and a brother and sister who learn how get rid of junk from an old aunt. Recommended for kidz ages 12-16. **Author:** Mark Wilkins **ASIN:** B0717B6SQ4

ASIN: B078JMR7ZB (Spanish Edition)

School Kidz Volume 2 High School   SP
9 stories about kids who are in high school. Within its pages you will meet a group of Kidz who get involved in a rotten egg war, a girl who doesn't exist, and a kid who sends a friend on a date with his sister. Recommended for kidz ages 14-18. **Author:** Mark Wilkins **ASIN:** B071W5WZZN

Coming Soon E Workbooks and an E Textbook!
A series of mini and one comprehensive E Textbook Under the title of Mr. Wilkins Teaches English by Mark Wilkins

The specific mini textbooks will be on topics such as Reading and Responding to Literature, and Methods for Writing Paragraphs and Essays. The Comprehensive text will include a weekly spelling component and both the mini texts and comprehensive Text will include creative lessons that promote creativity and critical thinking in students while fitting into common core standards. The mini texts will be no more than 99 cents each and the comprehensive text will be paperback for under $10!

All of the books are freshly created and contain exclusive intellectual property you won't find in any other texts. These books are perfect for students learning high school English levels 9 & 10 whether you are a classroom teacher or are home schooling your child. We are making the commitment to keep all of the books at low prices to allow parents and school districts to afford texts in the face of shrinking educational budgets. Purchasers will be given an opportunity to receive an email with a printable version of the exercises and assignments as well as links to online testing free of charge.

Author: Mark Wilkins   **ISBN:**   **ASIN:**

Compelling Stories for Adaptation to Short Film
For Film Students

Compelling stories in a set location with six or less characters. Easily adaptable to screenplay with notes on adapting them.
Author: Mark Wilkins   **ISBN:**   **ASIN:**

Loveforce Paperbacks

All of our paperback books cost between $6.50 and $7.50.

Stories of The Supernatural: A Storyteller Series Book SP Loveforce Duo

This collection of 15 stories is filled with ghosts, demonic creatures, monsters and death. It will haunt you, thrill you and entertain you. Within its pages you will marvel at the exploits of The Soul Collector and the uniqueness of Life Lines and Cannibal Money. You will shudder at the mention of a lump of coal or the dreaded Bungadun of Blood Valley and ride the rails on the ghost train. Strap on your seat belts, it's going to be a bumpy ride! **Author:** Mark Wilkins

ISBN-13: 978-1936462537   ISBN-13: 978-1936462575 SP

Karma   SP

Karma is the story of one man who negotiates between two different cultures, and opposing life views competing for his attention. His conflicts and struggles are overshadowed by cosmic forces he cannot understand. Karma provides insights into the struggles and conflicts we all face.

Author: Mark Wilkins   ISBN-13: 978-1936462506
ISBN-13: 978-1936462582 SP

A Week's Worth of Fiction Volumes 1 & 2
SP   Loveforce Duo

Whether it's people on the edges of society or Science Fiction Stories, this collection of Volumes 1 & 2 of A Week's Worth of Fiction gives you 2 volumes each with 7 stories that will thrill you, surprise you and make you think. Often dystopic and sometimes surreal, if you want stories you will never forget you only need to count to 7 and you can do it twice in this special paperback edition.

Author: Mark Wilkins   ISBN-13: 978-1936462551

Totally Outrageous Stories! Outrageous Satire
Loveforce Trio

There is absolutely nothing that escapes ridicule in this flagrantly outrageous, biting satire of everything you can imagine. This smart, flippant book pokes fun at the entertainment industry, the medical establishment, politics, societal norms, history and science. If you want to laugh to humor with no mercy, you have to get totally outrageous!
Author: Mark Wilkins   ISBN-10: 1936462494   ISBN-13: 978-1936462490

Slices of Life: Stories of Humor and Pathos (A Storyteller Series)   SP Loveforce Duo

Slices of Life Slices is a collection of humorous short stories about life. Most of them deal with marriage and family members. There are smart spouses, intelligent little children, guys trying to impress their friends and in-laws trying to master technology. Ignorance is the main theme of this book, ignorance that has consequences that are sometimes touching but always humorous. Each story is like a little slice of life but together, they make up an irresistible pie. Sit back, grab a cup of coffee and enjoy some slices of life because, before you know it, you will have finished the whole thing.
Author: Mark Wilkins   **ISBN-13: 978-1936462452   ISBN-13: 978-1936462469 SP**

Public School Confessions: Stories From The Front Lines of Public Education Loveforce Duo SP

Teachers, students and administrators come to life and often clash in dozens of stories from the front lines of public education. Within these pages you will meet people who are smart, rebellious and over caffeinated. Some stories will make you laugh, some will make you cry but they will also entertain you and make you think. **Author:** Mark Wilkins **ISBN-13: 978-1936462056   ISBN-13: 978-1936462063 SP**

The Faith Trilogy   SP   Loveforce Trio

This Faith Trilogy Paperback includes three faith filled books: What Faith Has Taught Me, The Best Quotes About God and Inspiration for All: Selected Inspirational Writings. **Author:** Mark Wilkins **ISBN-10**: 1936462516 **ISBN-13**: 978-1936462513

The Agnostic Faith Trilogy   SP   Loveforce Trio

Three great books combined in one paperback book! You get: Finding God without Religion, The Best Spiritual Quotes and Finding god in a Chaotic World. **Author:** The Prophet of Life
ASIN: **ASIN:**
(Spanish Edition)

Black in America

Black in America is an exploration of racism in America through essays and poems. It spans from the beginnings of the civil rights movement through today, It includes powerful new poems "Why We Say Black Lives Matter", "Baltimore", "Requiem for Laquan" It takes a look at people who have been lightning rods for race relations in America and has some surprising insights into the people and events that have shaped race relations in America for the past 60 years. It is a powerful work that teaches as it entertains and allows the reader gain new insights.
Author: The Prophet of Life
ISBN-13: 978-1936462025

Controversies
           SP

What do Caitlyn Jenner, Donald Trump, Hollywood Sex Scandals, a cure for AIDS, Chinese hackers, Adolf Hitler and Global Warming have in common? They are all at the heart of a controversy and there are stories about them in this unique book that turns tabloid headlines inside out.

Author: Mark Wilkins **ISBN-13:** 978-1936462483

www.ingramcontent.com/pod-product-compliance
Lightning Source LLC
Chambersburg PA
CBHW051647040426
42446CB00009B/1009